# The essential guide to owning, riding and maintaining…

# dirt *bikes!*

By Tory Briggs

Mixed *MEDIA*
2226 Eastlake Avenue East, Suite 69
Seattle, WA 98102
www.mm411.com

# MIXED *MEDIA* PRODUCTION TEAM

## Publisher
*Tom Mehren*

## Editing
*Patrick Duff*
*Gregory Maust*
*Connie Adams*

## Additional Editing Assistance
*Chelsea Piel, David Preston, James Boltz*

## Layout & Design
*Tom Mehren*
*Patrick Duff*

## Photography
*Front cover: Mike Urquhart*
*Interior pages and back cover: Tory Briggs*

## Photo Editing
*Tom Mehren*

## Printing
*Gorham Printing, WA*

# Table of Contents

# Foreword

Writing this book was a blast. If it works as intended, you can pick it up, follow it carefully and all by yourself achieve a successful launch into the world of dirt bike riding as a confident beginner. You'll have the right bike, gear, equipment, know the lingo, be able to take basic care of it all and most importantly, have learned the basic riding techniques needed to safely engage in this incredible sport.

From there, how you progress is up to you, but you can expect it to be fun and rewarding all the way.

There is a ton of information in here and I recommend that you read it all the way through, then keep it handy as a constant reference. Better yet, and quite likely, you will have someone more experienced available to be your guide on the start of this journey. Still, read the book first and if you can, get your guide to read it too, at least the riding lesson chapters. Insist that they, at least for those lessons, follow it as they teach you. The process I have described has been proven time and again to be successful. You'd be amazed at the spectrum of ages and physical capabilities that have quickly gotten over the beginner's hump using these methods.

I had another use in mind as well for parents desiring to get their offspring started in this sport. Your child may be too young to read or comprehend the book, but it is designed to make you an effective teacher and guide.

Now, as in any subject, everyone has an opinion. Dirt bike riders, being an especially independent and self-reliant lot, have plenty of them. I have no doubt that some details I have written about will be soundly renounced by some riders. That's okay; *viva la différence*. But I am confident that few if any will reject the advice and methods I recommend for learning how to ride the bike.

My goal is simple, I want to make your entry into this sport as easy, painless and inexpensive as possible (avoiding all the lessons

I learned the hard way). I sincerely wish you at least half the joy and pride I have felt over my forty years of dirt bike riding.

Lastly, I want to thank everyone I have ever interacted with regarding this sport over the years: those who freely shared their knowledge and tips, everyone who let me try their bikes, volunteers who have worked to preserve and enhance dirt biking, those who helped me out of jams both riding and mechanically induced and everyone I have ever ridden or raced with. You all helped create this book.

Happy trails!

# Introduction

## Why Ride a Dirt Bike?

*A group of ladies pause before heading out for a long loop.*

Hopefully that's a moot question! Something got your attention, maybe the bug has already bitten with a first ride, or the draw came from watching others ride, or more likely, listening to them talk about it afterward. Regardless, there are plenty of great reasons to ride besides that urge that won't let go.

Whether it's for the thrill, the exercise, the adventure, the challenge, the camaraderie, the freedom, to compete, getting away from it all or the family-oriented benefits, dirt biking offers them all, in whatever combinations and ratios you desire every time you ride!

The actual act of riding a dirt bike requires input from every part of you. Few other sports or activities simultaneously need all your strength, your most delicate touch, your instant animal-based reactions and your most acute thinking and decision making. Not only is your entire being involved, as you move across varied off-road terrain, it all must stay engaged in a constant flow.

Dirt biking can satisfy a thirst for exploration, a competitive drive and provide real stress relief from the intensity of modern life. On a bike, a rider, even one not able to hike well, can get deep into back country for the views, to commune with nature, to replenish the spirit. What might take a week on foot, time not available to most, a rider can cover in a day. It also seems that many dirt bike riders are naturally competitive and over the decades every form of racing or demonstration of skill has evolved and been perfected into events and series.

You'll soon find that most dirt bike riders think that their fellow riders are the best people on earth. They are self-sufficient, can-do, make-it-happen people. They would never abandon a fellow rider and will help a perfect stranger get back to camp or safety, even if it sidetracks their plans.

## Is This Something For My Family?

Absolutely! You'll be amazed by the benefits, many of which are true for any activity you all participate in. The difference may be how avidly a family is involved. Sure, dad's a coach and mom's a team manager and Jimmy and Suzy play soccer on the team, but the dirt bike riding family is out doing it together. The anticipation, preparation, travel and final readiness are all shared. Challenges, thrills, views, nature exploration, competition by class, tip sharing, pushing each other - the dirt biking family experiences these together.

I know just how much it has meant to my family. Each of us set our own goals in this sport and we all support each other's pursuit of them. We watched our children learn the importance of maintenance and mechanical know how and experience motor vehicle judgment and see the safe driving records they have on the streets since. Perhaps most importantly, we saw them learn to never give up, to compete fairly but intensely, to be a good sport and to leave the race at the track. Yes, the sport has also exposed this family to dozens and dozens of other families that are just the sort of folks you'd want to have your family around. The ensuing friendships are lifelong.

## What About Quads and ATVs?

No argument, the scene is very similar. Indeed, while this is a book about dirt biking, much of the material transfers directly to the four-wheeled, single-person all-terrain vehicle world.

## Taking Responsibility

One of the core themes within this sport is taking responsibility. Only you can be sure that your machine is in good operating condition. Only you can be sure you have gas in the tank, oil in the engine and air in the tires. Only you can know if any nuts and bolts need to be tightened, if the chain needs to be adjusted or that the air cleaner is not clogged.

It goes beyond taking responsibility for the bike. Only you can make sure to wear all of your safety equipment every time you ride. Only you can decide how far to twist the throttle, when to shift or how much brake to apply. Only you can choose to attempt to climb that hill or start over that steep drop. Only you can decide whether to attempt that big jump or to slam through the whoops.

Dirt bike riders rarely if ever are part of the sue-happy, litigious portion of the general public. We choose to ride, we choose when and where to ride, we choose what to ride and we don't blame anyone but ourselves when something goes wrong. We know that we can hurt ourselves riding, but we wear the safety gear, keep our bike in great shape and use our head. We know that only our actions are keeping our dirt bike from tipping over and we know that we will crash, eventually. We know that even though we have been clearing that 45' double effortlessly all day that all it takes is a tiny error and we won't clear it, with painful and/or expensive results.

We take responsibility for riding a dirt bike. We don't blame others for what might go wrong. Even when we race, especially when we race, we know that we can run into each other or roost each other, knock each other down, or simply perform a pirouetting lipskid all by ourselves.

Sure, you can think of scenarios where someone else's negligence or intent causes you to crash and injure yourself. But in reality, you are still responsible. You went riding or racing in the first place and only you can decide if the conditions and the scene are right for you.

Being fully responsible for yourself and your actions and any outcome that may occur is at the core of what makes riding a dirt bike one of the finest activities you can choose to participate in on the face of the planet. Being absolutely, completely, 100% responsible for yourself is the definition of freedom. Ask any dirt biker why they ride and they'll get to that free feeling right away, even if he/she can't quite put it into words. The real connection is the total freedom of being completely responsible for yourself.

Oh, and part of being responsible for yourself is not denying that you could get hurt, maybe a tiny bit, maybe a lot. If you get hurt, can you pay your medical bill? Do you have insurance instead? Are you prepared to miss some work if your injury forces that? Taking responsibility means taking this into consideration as you choose what, where, when and how to ride your dirt bike.

Finally, you can become permanently injured or crippled. Few riders ever die at this sport; it is probably more dangerous to fly a kite. I have never known a dirt biker to be bitter about blowing out a knee or ending up in a wheelchair. To every one, young or old, there is an easily expressed remembrance of what it is like to be truly alive - to be free.

I rode with a Vietnam Vet once. He had been a rising star in Southern California motocross before getting drafted. A land mine took his right foot, part of his left and all the fingers on his right hand except stumps where his thumb and forefinger had been. He knew what could make him truly happy in spite of his loss, figured out how to get the brake lever and throttle over to the left side of the bars, stuffed the missing space in his boot and went riding every chance he could get. A lot of riders would be very surprised to discover just how much he had overcome to keep riding - if they weren't also embarrassed at not being able to keep up with him.

You choose to ride, or do anything else in this life you've been given to live, so follow through and take responsibility for your choices. You'll realize soon enough that all dirt bike riders seem to live by this simple creed. Maybe that's why you'll also soon be saying that dirt bike riders are the finest people on earth; the kind of people you want to hang with, that you want your children to have as examples and that you would want to have around in an emergency.

# CHAPTER 1:

## *DIRT BIKE RIDING OPPORTUNITIES*

Before we get into bike types and selection, buying riding gear and learning to ride, let's take a quick spin around the basic types of riding experience.

### Just Playing

Give me but a tiny parcel of dirt and a dirt bike and I'll have a blast. Make it a bigger chunk and the wahoo factor multiplies. Anything thrown in - a ditch, a hill, a twisting trail or a mound with jump faces is worthy of riding over 873 times just to ride. Two guys on twenty-year-old 50s will go at it around a 35 foot oval until dark, unless they have headlights or can line up the pickup's lights, or the moon is full enough, or until one, no make that both bikes, quit running.

Play riding can be two bikes running side-by-side on a two-track to anywhere. Flying, but staying smooth; total trust between the riders; willing to lay it down rather than force the other into the weeds in a corner hit too hot, enthralled by the resonant hum of the engines.

You might spend an hour trying to learn to do a wheelie, stoppie or rail a berm. Maybe all riding is really play riding at heart: just having fun on the motorcycle. But there are special types of play riding.

### Trail Riding (motorized hiking)

Hiking is great. You get exercise, enjoy nature, see splendid vistas and find solitude. Trail riding is motorized hiking and trail riders seek the same thing on their bikes as they do when they hoof it, pedal it or let the horse carry it. Motorized hiking is a boon, giving range to those with limited time and mobility to those who can't walk far. It could take two days on foot to reach that certain spot you need to enjoy for a while whereas you can get there and back in one hour on your bike.

Trail riders work loops or long out-and-backs. The familiar stuff offers a chance to boogie, but the need to explore seems to run deep in us. Some groups have a pecking order, some rotate point duty, some forever compete for it. Regardless, they take care of each other holding up for the next rider in line at unfamiliar intersections. They stop for the scenery, bask in the camaraderie and find special places to refresh their souls. Don't limit your vision of trails to wooded terrain, this form of riding works everywhere.

*Pausing for a spectacular view on a high mountain ridge.*

Trail riding is play riding at heart, but it has a little more purpose and focus. You'll find trail riders who are incredibly serious about their form of play riding with bikes that started life designed with trails in mind and have been refined and customized to the nth degree. Their fanny packs are a marvel of spare pieces, trick tools and human survival ingenuity. There might be real exploration, with maps and GPS units, seeking traces of long-lost routes into the hinterlands.

Every dirt biker goes trail riding. It may best express the freedom, the soaring or magic carpet sensation, of the ultimate one-person all-terrain transportation system - dirt bike riding.

## Organized Events

By definition, if Peter calls up Paul and they plan to go play riding or trail riding, it is an organized event. There are plenty of formally organized events, too - poker runs, dual sport rides, local club play days and more. While these are great ways to learn the ropes at an unfamiliar riding area and meet new riding partners, they also attract regular crowds of entrants who love the scene.

*Poker Run riders enjoying the trail*

These are almost always trail rides with arrowed routes or maps. The route is open for a few hours in the morning and you leave when you are ready. "Closing" it gives the last out time to finish the loop before the awards ceremony. The chase (usually called sweep) riders get those with bike problems home. Along with the main, family loop, there is often an "ironman" option with a completely different loop or extra sections containing harder riding challenges that break off from and rejoin the main route. Short, easy, close to the staging area youth loops ensure that these events have something for everyone in the family  Usually the host club has obtained a pile of dirt bike goodies from the area shops to give away after the event and coveted event t-shirts are common.

In a poker run, cards are drawn at checkpoints with the last card at the finish and trophies or goodies are given away from the best hand until the prizes are depleted. Somehow a very young rider "manages" to get four of a kind… these are casual family events after all.

## Competition

There's a type of competition for every type of riding, every type of dirt bike, every class and every age group. Hare Scrambles, Motocross, Enduros, Supercross, ISDE's, Arenacross, Flat Track, EnduroCross, Trials, Supermotard, GNCC's, Hare-n-Hounds, Ice Racing, Desert, Cross Country and Cross-Continent to name a few. If there is a way to race, we will.

Some riders focus entirely on one facet of competition and rarely, if ever, ride except to practice or compete. Others dabble in as many types as possible. A few make a living at racing but the great majority just race because they love to. Amateur racing is huge and it is the foundation without which pro racing could not exist. Racing is just about every bit as serious at any level whether battling for first or tenth. Racing friendships, even between on-track rivals, can be lifelong.

If you ride a dirt bike you'll probably race a lot without ever entering an organized event. You'll chase your buddies down the trail or try to keep them from catching you. You'll dice around at the track. You'll find a jillion ways to play race if you look for them and not all happen on the bike. There are certainly more total minutes spent just play racing than at all formal events.

*The first turn of a competition event, courtesy of the AA class.*

## Play Racing

You can make this extremely fun and intense practice all at once. The theme is simple: the slower rider goes first and maintains the best pace they can. The faster rider has to make a clean, non-blocking pass, then pull over safely and do it again. The slower rider is learning much: staying focused ahead, holding lines, braking late, gear selection, faultless shifting and acceleration. The faster rider is learning alternate lines, judging what a slower rider will do and taking advantage of fleeting opportunities to pass.

Using lap times or seat-of-the-pants judgment a whole moto can be set up with all the play racers staggered around the course, the intention being that if everyone rides perfectly to their current potential all would get to the finish line at the same time. Try it, it's a blast.

*The author's son and a family friend play racing.*

## Where Can I Ride?

Okay, with perhaps an idea of how you'll be intending to spend your time in the saddle, let's unfold the map and scope out where we can ride. The critical issue of sound is introduced in this chapter, as well as an overview of the basic land use issue (politics) forever pressuring our sport toward extinction.

As far as dirt biking goes, there are only two types of land, public and private. You ride on either one or the other. Your riding is directly impacted by the political realities and management practices in play.

## Public Land

There are only two types of public land upon which you might ride your bike - federal or state.

Many states have formal, designated riding opportunities. Some of these are on state-owned land, others will be on federal property. These may be in the form of parks, trail networks or open riding areas.

Parks generally are centered around a motocross circuit or flat track oval and often include a youth track. There may be camping, different tracks for different ability levels, a hillclimb and other amenities.

Trail networks might be as simple as a single route ridden out and back only. Believe it or not, some states have exactly one such trail and no more! If you're lucky, there will be more than a few with marked trails and maps to help navigate. Usually there are easy, medium and difficult routes arranged in loops. These are typically maintained in a cooperative arrangement between the responsible land managers and local clubs where volunteers put in hard hours on the ground.

Open riding areas are typically desert or grasslands and you ride where you will. Trails and routes occur naturally, generally following the age-old steps of animals, indigenous peoples, explorers, trappers and miners.

The core reality of public land riding opportunities is that they are insufficient to meet the ever-growing demand. They tend to be shrinking over time, while the number of dirt bike riders and bikes continuously increases, causing remaining areas to be overused and stressing maintenance systems. Various factors are behind the steady loss, from funding to noise issues.

There is a trend indicating that in the near future this will be a private land sport.

We must ask - why? Primarily, a savvy minority numbering fewer than those who ride, operating out of often extreme environmental organizations, is dedicated to eradicating our sport (and any motorized or mechanized off-road recreation) from the face of the earth. Because they are able to conceal this aim within a greater environmental mission, they have access to Joe Public's mind, wallet and guilt, abetted by most mainstream press. With superior funding and a legal and legislative patience that understands driving desired change one little piece at a time, slicing salami so to speak, they have not only frozen growth of opportunity, they have steadily reduced the acreage on which we might ride.

What can you do? Join a local, a regional (Blue Ribbon Coalition) and a national (American Motorcycle Association) club, if for no more effect than to increase the political clout by one. Then participate in a letter campaign, volunteer for organizational, political or on-the-ground trail work. Put something into this sport that gives you so much.

## Private Land

One day our sport may be confined to private land opportunities. There is no doubt that well-heeled and organized enemies of motorized recreation are determined to achieve that goal (and then strive to take those away).

Private land may be as simple as your spacious back yard, or as immense as a private timber company's holdings. Also appearing across the country are businesses focused on providing deluxe riding opportunities. You can find these advertised in local and national publications. Besides tracks and/or trails, some offer group packages including meals, schools and bunkhouse accommodations.

It is a shame that all public lands cannot be managed like the most progressive private forests. I have seen where resource and mineral extraction are accomplished hand-in-hand with dispersed camping, designated areas for bikes, horses, hikers, quads and 4WDs and successful big game (elk, for example) herd recovery programs.

How the enemies of off-road recreation can maintain with a straight face that there is not enough public land in this great country of ours to provide properly-managed resource extraction, ample recreation and ecosystem protection is beyond me.

Small scale private property riding, such as your own acreage, carries special responsibilities. Bottom line, you must realize that you can severely damage our sport by failing to interact with your neighbors properly. Controlling sound is primary, but so are dust, amount and timing of use and any other impacts that can cross over your property line. And even if you think you have it all under control, communication is critical. You must make sure that you listen to your neighbors! Tell them they can halt your use at any time should it conflict with an event they are hosting. Mismanaged dirt bike riding can create conflict. Don't add bullets to our enemy's arsenal!

## Tracks

Tracks are a specific form of private land riding. They range from limited club scenarios to businesses open to the general riding public. In colder and wetter regions, indoor track businesses are appearing and, in some cases, thriving.

Many offer at least both a main and a youth circuit. Track riding is a good way to use repetition to improve skills. Tracks also include jumps, whoops and other technical obstacles that may not be suitable for a beginner.

*An example of a track scenario. This one is private, requiring an annual membership to ride. There are no competitive events and members share in maintenance. As is typical, this one has a small youth circuit to go along with the main track.*

There may also be a significant spectrum of riding skills present on the track at any given time including expert level riders flying over everything. You must be the judge of your capabilities and never attempt to transfer blame to the owners for anything that might happen. You come to ride and you know full well that you could hurt yourself. Key words – you could hurt yourself – even if that means that another rider hits you while you were in control and on line. It is not anyone else's fault.

## Trail Networks

These are designed, managed and maintained trail systems, most commonly on public land. Some states have none, some have only one token area and some offer a wide array. It all depends on the state, its history with ORVs and the extent to which dirt bike riders band together and work with communities and government.

Local shops, clubs or Ranger district offices can direct you and some will even provide trail maps. It is usually easy to hook up with other riders - start at the trailhead! You'll also find that there is never enough money or manpower to maintain the trails, fix wear, clear windfall, build new sections, and that there are plentiful opportunities to volunteer and put some sweat equity back into your sport. Do it! At the least, when you ride, stick to the trails - no short cuts – and be gentle on the throttle through soft sections. Take care of them like you built them yourself. If you ever do build a section, you'll understand.

Open areas like deserts also have trail networks, less confined and more likely to be spider-webbed with routes. Think about it, stick to the existing trails even in an area like this and don't make new routes indiscriminately. There are plenty of them! You'll be helping to keep the area open. Manage the area by managing your riding.

Not all trail areas are motorized only, they may be used by hikers and horses, too. And remember they may be used by quads and 4WDs and other vehicles you'd want to pay attention to. When you encounter other users, avoid conflict and pass each other in a friendly manner. Pull over, slow down, stop and chat. Blowing by and making folks think they have to jump off the trail for their own safety, will be reported as conflict. Land managers have to act on conflict and you are likely to be responsible for the conversion of an area from multiple use to hiking only.

Encountering horses on the trail requires a specific response. Pull off the trail and shut off the motorcycle. Remove your helmet so that the animals can see that you are a person. Follow the requests the riders may make. Backcountry horsemen have their own land use battles and regularly ally with us to protect multiple use trail systems.

## Sound

There is one aspect of dirt bike riding that absolutely can cause conflict, as legally recognized by the courts - sound. Complaints about it can and do cause land closures.

*Sound measurement: The official method includes specified rpm for each brand/displacement, typically 50% of redline. The gentleman kneeling down to the left is holding a vibration-driven tachometer against the engine as he controls the throttle with his right hand. The gentleman on the right is holding a sound meter 20" from the end of the pipe, 45 degrees off the centerline of the bike, at the same height as the end of the silencer and, most importantly, the meter is square to the angled measuring stick, not the centerline of the bike, such that it is actually pointing slightly behind the bike.*

In a strange twist of fate, we solved this problem back in the 80s. Folks quit running un-muffled bikes. Sound tests were common - too loud meant no entry. Bikes got quieter year-to-year. Then, the new wave of high performance four-stroke motorcycles led to the need for a new wave of education and enforcement. Critically, the lower sound frequency of a four stroke travels further. So we had to start all over to educate new riders, reinstitute sound testing and pressure the manufacturers into providing quiet technology. It is working again. No matter what - keep it quiet!

## Spark Arrestors

The spark arrestor is a device intended to prevent sparks or glowing material from being ejected out the exhaust of a dirt or dual sport bike. They are required on a great deal of public land including all federal land. The fines for not having one can run over a hundred dollars.

You need to find out if your bike has one. Almost all stock silencers, if equipped with a spark arrestor, have a clearly-stamped inscription to that effect. Your dealer or used bike seller should know and have no problem telling you about the bike you're thinking of making yours.

If it doesn't have one and you'll be spending time on public land, or even private land that has fire potential, you might have a few choices. First is to simply purchase an aftermarket silencer/spark arrestor combo, if your manufacturer doesn't already offer one. If your manufacturer does, convert your bike back to the stock pipe. Some allow conversion between spark arrested or not. There are bolt-on spark arrestors that attach to the end of your existing silencer which can be considerably less expensive, but much more difficult to mount securely.

The designs tend to employ either a screen with holes sized so that only sparks deemed too small to be threatening can escape, or a design which spins or twirls the exhaust gases so as to force the sparks out into trap areas of the unit. The screens can and will clog and generally have to be burned clean with a torch.

The typical enforcement test, if no spark arrestor stamping is found or if tampering or lack of maintenance is suspected, is to attempt to insert a stick or straightened clothes hanger or similar wire up the exhaust, expecting to encounter either the screen or the centrifugal section blocking the way within the silencer body.

# CHAPTER 2

## *GETTING GEARED UP*

Okay, already! Master and apply everything in the next three chapters and you will have all you need to be a dirt bike rider. Yes, a beginner, but one who is off to a solid start, who will blend in quickly with the overall scene and who will improve at an accelerated rate.

These chapters proceed from assessing critical pre-requisites for the rider to the actual steps of learning to operate the controls and thus ride the bike. The topics are:

**Riding Gear** – Start wearing it all from day one. What are all of the elements of a full set of gear, how do you put it on and get it clean?

**The Dirt Bike** – Identify the major parts and all of the controls.

**Choosing a Bike** – Your learning experience will be much better with the right machine.

**Other Stuff You'll Need, Have to Do, or Want** – Gas cans, mixing two stroke fuel, stickers and more.

**Critical Pre-requisites** – Is the student ready, able to ride a bicycle well and otherwise physically capable? Is there a suitable bike and location?

**Learning To Ride** – Progressing from gaining trust in your brakes to operating the shifter, then starting the bike, starting to finesse the clutch, starting and stopping, moving on to higher gears and skill development drills.

Master the above and you can ride a motorcycle. You're still a newbie and have much to learn, but most of what you don't know requires you to put hours on the bike to acquire, so you are over the hump and on your way.

After the detailed chapters that lead you through the learning steps outlined above, you'll find drills which will grow your skill level, along with lots of tips about stuff you'll need to support your new addiction and how to keep your bike running properly. Ride on!

## Riding Gear

Don't even think about slinging a leg over your bike without wearing all of the available riding gear. Think of it all as essential safety equipment. Remember, you not only can, but will, fall down. You'll be more protected than an NFL middle linebacker, though and you'll bounce right up unhurt from most of your soil sampling expeditions.

*Protected head-to-toe; don't ever ride without all your gear!*

Most riding gear manufacturers offer both men's, women's and youth styles and sizes. Female riders have gotten by okay over the years by simply wearing the standard men's issue, but both sexes seem to appreciate the better fit of the new stuff. There is an incredible array of styles and colors available, tending toward bold and bright. Sometimes it can be hard to find more subdued hues, but they are out there.

There are a few things you shouldn't wear. Punt the jewelry, bracelets, fancy watch, necklaces, earrings and, if possible, piercings. If they don't hurt you, you'll probably lose them. Imagine grinding that silver ball above your right eyebrow into the ground. Same with rings; in the extreme you can even snag a band and take your finger off. Mounted stones on rings will get lost.

This list is presented in approximate order of importance. At an absolute minimum wear a helmet (or don't even get on the bike), eye protection, sturdy footwear, rugged pants such as denim and a long sleeved shirt. You'll pay the price if you don't. The basic price of riding without protective gear is scrapes. Big ones, measured in inches, that ooze and stick to bandages and bed sheets and grow crusty scabs. Your significant other will shun touching you. Your choice.

## Helmet (aka brain bucket, lid)

*There is a helmet for every budget, sense of style and color desire. Or you can always have someone airbrush a custom design for your lid.*

The body can survive a lot of abuse and injury. Bones can break and heal, but head injuries are another story. First, any cut to the head bleeds like crazy. Second, hard blows to the noggin can permanently impair, if not kill you. No matter what, purchase a good helmet and never ride the bike, not even for a quick test after a repair, without it. Most any helmet you can find on the market today meets safety standards, so choose based on fit, followed by price and style.

Go for a full face design with the integral face guard. An off-road model is generally lighter and cooler than a street model and accepts goggles better – the street models tend to supply a flip up visor, which does not work well off-road. There can be glare problems with a visor, but most importantly they do not keep dust out of your eyes like goggles can. If you must buy a used helmet, try to ensure that it is a name brand and doesn't look all banged up. As for fit, it should be snug, not overly tight and certainly not loose. The brain bucket won't do you much good if it makes you crash by wandering all over your head as you bounce through the boonies, blocking your vision and careening you into immovable obstacles, like your buddy's new truck. While wearing the helmet check to see if the cheek pads are in contact with your cheeks. You should also grab the helmet with your hands and try to rotate the helmet side to side and tilt it up and down. The helmet padding should pull your skin in the direction you are pulling, not slide over it. A new helmet will "loosen up" ever so slightly as it breaks in, so err on the side of slightly too snug.

*Use the straps to slightly spread the helmet open as you slip it on.*

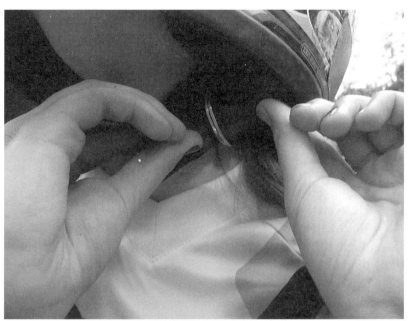

*Pass the untwisted strap through both metal rings.*

*Loop the strap around the second ring and back through the first, draw tight.*

To put it on, grasp the helmet on either side of the bottom opening by the two loose straps, pull on the straps so as to widen the hole a bit and slide the helmet over your head. It helps to have your hair pulled back; looking up so that your hair naturally falls back works. Remove any twists in the plain strap, the one without the two metal rings and pass it under your chin and through both rings on the other strap. Bring the end of the plain strap around the second ring, then between the two rings and back out of the center of the first ring. Try this with the helmet in your lap if you've never done it before. Pull the strap snug, but not so tight as to affect breathing. This looping of the straps through the rings creates a locking situation if you pull on the strap under your chin and a sliding/adjustable setup if you push on the loose end. To remove, push the loose end of the strap back into the rings to ease their grip and feed the strap back through the rings. Not all helmets have the same shape inside, so try several on. Many designs have removable, washable liners, which you will soon learn to appreciate. There are usually vent systems designed to keep your head cool and wick moisture away. Some can be selectively opened and closed depending on conditions.

Years ago, a buyer needed to be concerned about the various levels (or lack of) safety certification as they shopped for a helmet. These days, you can count on all of the helmets at a reputable shop meeting minimum requirements. You can pay just over a hundred bucks for a basic model or up to hundreds of dollars. The more expensive offerings feature ultra light weight, better venting and flashy colors and graphics. You'll have no problem finding a local business specializing in custom paint jobs if you must express yourself with your own design.

Helmets have a useful life, which primarily depends on how many times and how hard they are asked to perform their prime function. When a helmet slams the ground hard, the materials in the shell and liner absorb energy to protect your skull, but this also renders those materials less able to do it again. Replace a helmet that has taken a hard blow.

Finally, some riders adhere to a superstition and make a scratch in their brand new helmet with a key before they ride with it on for the first time. Hmmm . . .

## Eye Protection

Protect your fragile peepers. Expect to find lots of stuff in the air as you ride, with much of it seemingly determined to hit you in the face. Roost (the dirt and rocks flung rearward from the spinning tire on the bike in front of you), insects of all varieties, branches, dust and even low flying birds (don't laugh; I've almost taken one in the face) will all target your eyeballs. Above/around fifty mph, just the air pressure alone will make your eyes water and blind you. Goggles are the best solution; they are comfortable, shock resistant and designed to create a dust-blocking seal while maximizing visibility. If you wear glasses, every manufacturer offers a style with the needed extra room for your frames. There are companies that specialize in merging your prescription lenses and goggles into a single assembly.

To put goggles on smoothly, hold them in front of your face and flip the strap, without any twists, to the lens side of them. Position the goggles against your face and flip the strap up and over the top of the helmet. Slide your hand under the strap to be sure there are no uncool twists where the strap passes around the back of the helmet.

Costs are reasonable, ranging from not much over twenty bucks to several times that. Basic lenses are clear and that is the best choice for most riders. If you will be dealing with bright sunlight or glare, there are tinted lenses available.

If you don't have to deal with dust and choose to take a risk and simply wear your prescription glasses, or sun glasses, at least be smart enough to make sure they are impact resistant/shatter proof.

*Flip the strap over, place the goggles against your face.*

*Bring the strap up and over your visor and voilà, no twists.*

## Gloves

There are plenty of reasons to wear gloves when you ride. They cushion your hands as you grip handlebars, prevent chafing and lessen blisters. It won't always be warm when you ride and numb fingers will refuse to respond on the controls with the speed and precision needed. Most of all, when you do find yourself separating from your bike and headed for a tussle with the ground and naturally put your hands out to break your fall (umm, don't do this unless going very slowly toward terra firma—better to tuck and roll), you'll appreciate how they tend to keep your skin attached to your palms.

*Glove colors, fabrics and styles abound*

Riding gloves come in a huge array of styles and colors. Soft materials are used in the palm area and tougher fabrics on the back of the hand and fingers. Some designs are pre-shaped in the position your hands will be in as you hold on to the bars on your bike. Make sure they fit well; not too tight or too loose. Too small and the gloves will impede circulation in your hands, making it harder to operate the controls. Too large will result in the material bunching near the knuckles and creating blisters on your palms.

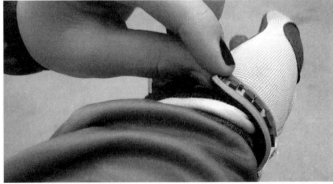

*Don't tighten any wrist strap at all – you'll cut off vital circulation.*

Ease your gloves off and on; the seams between the different materials will last longer. On designs that include some kind of wrist strap, usually fastened by Velcro, do not tighten these at all, fasten them loosely so that there is no constriction around the wrists. Cutting off circulation to the hands, even a tiny bit, will increase dreaded arm pump. Arm pump, which can actually be painful enough to force you to stop riding, is a circulation/nerve issue caused by extended clenching of the hands coupled with tensed forearm muscles. If you experience arm pump, you will know it by the pain sensation and a loss of control of your hands. Stop riding, the condition will clear up shortly. Relax your hands and forearms; gently shaking your hands and opening/closing them in a loose fist seems to speed up the recovery.

## Kidney Belt

*No lack of style or comfort choice amongst kidney belts.*

What's a kidney belt, you ask, something to help you hold your bladder on a long ride? Not quite, but it is an essential piece of dirt bike safety equipment, designed to perform two critical tasks. First it provides lower back penetration protection, where relatively unprotected vitals like your kidneys are located. But even if you never crash, your organs in that slim and trim gut of yours were not designed to absorb the shock and motion of dirt biking. The belt works to keep your organs snug and together, free from internal chafing. I can personally attest to both attributes. Do yourself a favor and don't learn the value of a kidney belt the hard way.

Kidney belts are simply wide elastic belts worn between the hips and the ribs. Some wear them inside, some outside, of their jerseys. They are fastened by good old Velcro. Make it snug; don't try to improve your profile by tightening it like a girdle. Like goggles, these run from around twenty bucks to several times that.

*The rigid or stiffer part of the belt goes around your back, the Velcro straps come around the front.*

## Boots

Dirt bike footwear are called motocross boots and they are awesome. You could kick down a door, or tromp a small car into junk without feeling a thing. As you accumulate hours on your bike, you will kick lots of things heavier and bigger without ever intending to and you'll be glad you wear them. You probably won't last ten miles in tennis shoes without severely injuring your foot.

Yes, you can perhaps wear a less expensive hiking style boot, but beware. You do not want a square edge to the heel, so take a knife or saw and cut a nice angled ramp on the front, leading edge. If you don't, you will catch that square heel on a firmly planted rock and kick yourself in the butt so hard as to raise a welt and leave a bruise, if you don't also hyperextend your knee right on to the surgeon's table. This alternative must also be the tall type that comes at least halfway up your calf, so as to provide some ankle support and protection.

*If you can afford it, you can have as many different mx boots as Imelda Marcos had shoes. Well, almost.*

There is a wide range of boots available. Try on as many pairs in your price range as you can. You should be able to find a pair in basic black for not too much over a hundred dollars and you certainly can pay several times that for the latest hot models. Actual size vs. "manufacturer's size" can vary significantly and so does the interior shape. New boots can be stiff, although the latest designs don't seem to require walking around the house in them all week to break them in like the good old days. The strap-buckle fasteners are generally over-center cams so as to lock in place when closed. Your salesperson will be glad to demonstrate. The fasteners are easily adjustable. Don't reject a brand unaware of this, thinking they don't fit. You will also want to wear moto socks, (heavy designs which cover your entire calf), as you make your size selection.

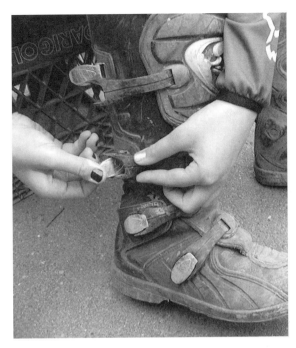

*The lever goes through the hole in the strap, the end of the strap is placed in a slot in the lever and the lever is rotated, which leverages the strap tight, until it snaps in its holder.*

How tight to adjust? This will come down to personal preference, but you might start with these notions. Obviously, avoid any buckle being so tight as to be painful or constrict circulation. I tend to ensure that the toe region and the top of the boot are adjusted on the tight side, while the middle buckles are on the loose side for ankle flexibility. For shifting and braking, you want the boot to be one with your foot for the greatest control and finesse. Keeping the top buckle firm will help keep your knee pads in place and resist water and mud getting in from the top. Looser adjustments in the middle will help you bend and be flexible at the ankle.

As for water and mud, motocross boots are waterproof. Treating them with appropriate sealants can only help. For a particularly wet ride, many will wrap duct tape around the top of the boot, taping the boot to their pants. There are also "gators" on the market for this purpose that are available through outdoor stores.

## Shoulder Pads

An NFL linebacker isn't as well protected as a properly outfitted dirt bike rider. A set of shoulder pads provides an array of protective functions: absorbing the force of impacts, deflecting roost, protecting against puncture and minimizing the risk of breaking the delicate clavicle (collar bone).

*Given the colors and styles, you'll probably choose to wear your shoulder pads on the outside.*

The basic design concept utilizes vented plastic shell pieces connected by straps and suspended slightly away from the body with webbing, the shape and overlapping of the shells. There is generally a chest and a back panel, the latter longer to provide additional lower back protection, shoulder pieces and upper arm sections. The main body shells are slotted for ventilation and backed with foam for comfort.

*Snap the side buckles together and adjust the straps to keep the front and rear panels comfortably close to your torso.*

Don the pads by slipping them over your head, with the smaller panel in front. Slip each arm through the loop at the end of each arm section. Last, fasten the straps at the lower part of each side. All the straps will be adjustable.

Wearing them under or over the jersey is a long-unsettled style question. If you choose under, be sure to get an oversized jersey. Prices start well under a hundred dollars and go up to about double that. If you've picked up on a theme here, they are available in a full array of colors. There are some fringe designs, like padded body armor intended to be worn under a normally sized jersey. There are also extreme protection designs for the youngest riders.

## Elbow Pads

Your elbows and forearms will often be the first thing to hit the ground when you crash and a slide along the dirt will grind off huge patches of skin in a microsecond if you rely only on a jersey. These wounds, sometimes called "raspberries," are a pain to deal with, sticking to everything—bandages, shirts and most unpleasantly, your sheets at night. The thin pads provided in some jersey designs simply won't protect you. Good protection can make the difference between a break, fracture or no damage to the bone at all. Ditto for the knee pads in your pants .

Elbow pads are an inexpensive solution. They are held on with elastic straps. Grab the cuff of your jersey as you slip them on, it'll help. If they start slipping down as you ride, pull more of your jersey through and they'll stay put. Make sure you don't select a size that are too tight and cut off circulation – remember, that can enhance arm pump.

## Pants

Back in the good old days, motocross pants were pure leather; hot, heavy, but tough as cow hide (duh), providing solid protection from a long grinding slide across terra firma. These days, you'll find leather in certain parts of some designs, but most use modern, tough, washable fabrics that are much lighter than leather and can "breathe." There are pads for your hips and, most importantly, knees. These have a shin piece and a hinged knee cup, all backed by foam for comfort. Some kneepad/pants combinations utilize a pocket inside the shin section, others use elastic straps or Velcro-fastened straps. Actually, neither are needed and some riders slice off or don't use the straps, to avoid cutting off any circulation at all. Your riding boots will trap the shin section of the pads nicely between the top front of the boot and your shin.

*Moto pants combine comfort, freedom of movement and, of course, a rainbow of styles and colors*

Today's modern fabrics allow every possible color, and pants and jerseys are typically sold as matched sets. Colors cover the rainbow and there are always designs intended to coordinate with the popular bike brands. It is actually hard for a conservative dresser to find a set in mellow, muted, even drab colors, but they're out there.

## Jersey

*The jersey is perhaps the core of each rider's gear style and color decision, and everything else can match if you wish.*

The jersey is simply your riding shirt; it must be long sleeved to protect your arms. The materials are tear resistant and many offer thin pads over the elbow and forearm. There are materials for various climates, vented, cotton, etc.

The jersey is a key focal point of a dirt bike rider's personal gear statement. The right motif is essential. Many have their name or nickname added across their shoulders and/or their riding number on the back.

## Under It All

Boxers or briefs? Considering that you will more than occasionally be bouncing the delicate zone on the seat, or worse, the tank, as you ride, boxers are out. You want some support, for sure. Briefs aren't so great, either; sweaty cotton can really chafe, leading to a very uncomfortable situation dirt bike riders, especially those who sit down too much when they ride, called "monkey butt." You'll look like an orangutan, walk like a grizzled cowboy and be none too eager to park it should you ever earn a dose.

The wise move is to spring for riding shorts. They're similar to bicycle riding gear, but we (have the decency to) wear them under other clothing. It's probably also wise to wear an athletic protective cup, but I've never known a single rider who did. I suspect that it is just too plain uncomfortable. You can thank me for no pictures in this section when we meet for a ride one day.

Ladies, wear an appropriate, supportive upper body undergarment.

## Neck Brace

*Simple horseshoe-shaped pads with Velcro straps, the neck brace is becoming more common (going from never to rarely but surely seen)*

In the past, you never saw riders wearing any sort of neck brace, but these days it is a growing trend. The only possibly usable design actually comes from kart and other four-wheeled racing, a simple horseshoe-shape with a Velcro strap fastener across the front. While one offers some neck protection, the lack of head mobility would be a drawback to consider. If at all, you might opt for one for a very young beginning rider.

## How Do I Get My Gear Clean?

Even if you never get to relive the childhood joy of playing in mud and truly coating every inch of your body in thick, gooey muck, you'll still stink up your gear with sweat. This is a truly athletic activity after all. Here are some tips to help you get it all looking like new and smelling fresh again.

Generally, all of the clothing parts of your gear can go right into the washer, including your pants and jersey, undergarments and your kidney belt, gloves and elbow pads, but check the labels. You'll want to fasten any Velcro, like on your belt and gloves, or you'll be peeling other clothing off it. Fasten all buckles and zip up zippers as well. Most use normal detergent and many riders swear that using the gentle or delicate cycle on the machine extends gear life. Do not use the dryer, unless it has an air only or a delicate/low setting. The synthetic materials or the graphics may shrink or melt! If you must get your gear dried quickly using a normal setting, watch it like a hawk, check it often and pull out each piece as it approaches being dry or seems to be getting hot. The best bet is to hang it up to dry.

If you never see mud, you'll obviously need to wash your gear less often. When you do get muddy, you might find it wise to pre-wash the muddiest stuff with the hose, knocking off the big chunks, or maybe pre-soaking it in a tub with some detergent. I shouldn't have to tell you how happy the lady of the house will be if your indiscretion with your mud-caked gear leads to stains in her delicates or a call to the repairman. I've never heard of a rider abusing a machine at the local laundromat either.

*Old abandoned highway cones make great boot wash-n-dry stands*

Boots will have to be washed with the hose or pressure washer. The trick method is to find a pair of abandoned highway marker cones, those rubber, orange ones. You'll find that your boots will fit nice and snug over the cone shape, but be careful to get the tip of the cone inside the expansion flap where the boots open wide in the front. You now have both a washing stand which will keep water out of the insides and a drying stand. I've also seen some custom drying racks made from plastic plumbing pipe, with ventilation holes drilled and the ability to blow hot air through it with a hair dryer. This is especially useful if you see lots of water in your rides and tend to soak your boots now and then. The dirt bike cleaning solutions will make them look like new with minimum effort.

If your helmet has a removable liner, follow the instructions that came with it. The shell should be wiped down with a mild soap. If your helmet's liner is not removable, just take it in the shower. Fill her up, squirt in some shampoo, lather, rinse, repeat. It may take a few cycles, you'll be surprised at how long it can take until it rinses clear. Towel out as much water as you can; it will take quite a while to dry. You can speed up the process with a hair dryer or by making sure it gets plenty of ventilation.

The main point in generally cleaning your goggles is to avoid scratching the lens. Don't touch the lenses until you've washed away as much dirt and dust as you can, and when you do use lots of water! The foam and strap will clean right up with a little soak in soapy water.

You don't have much choice but to spray wash shoulder pads. Don't forget that the bike cleaning solution will help here, too.

# CHAPTER 3

## *GETTING A BIKE*

Our next mission is to get you familiar with all of the major parts of your dirt bike.

### Engine

The motor. The powerplant. The heart of the machine. That big lump of metal right in the center of that dirt bike you're drooling over. Yeah, right there under the fuel tank. It's probably silver, or natural aluminum color or painted black.

Today's dirt bike engines are marvels of technology. Massive computer programs developed to model designs for the high dollar racing teams have been applied to the dirt bike world and we reap the benefits.

Except for a few exotic twins, the majority of our engines are single cylinder designs, meaning there is but one piston doing all the work. You'd be amazed at how tiny the piston is in a 50cc bike (about the size of your big toe) yet it can propel a full size adult along quite briskly. Yeah, dirt bike engine sizes are talked about in ccs (cc = cubic centimeter), rather than cubic inches, probably due to some marketing genius long ago who cringed at having to sell 1.5 cubic inchers.

*A big air-cooled four stroke. The tall engine (that valve train on top), the fins to assist air cooling and the skinny, relatively constant diameter exhaust pipe are your visual clues.*

*A tiny air-cooled four stroke. All that engine above the spark plug is where the valve train lives. Air cooling fins and the skinny pipe; she's a thumper.*

*A big, water-cooled four stroke. The lack of cooling fins (and radiators, not shown), tall cylinder and constant diameter pipe give it away.*

*A water-cooled four stroke from the other side, to emphasize the fairly constant diameter, relatively skinny pipe (compared to the widely varying shape of a two stroke's exhaust).*

*Perhaps one day to be a relic, banned by legislation, here's a water-cooled two stroke. Notice the short, squat cylinder and the spark plug right on top of the engine. There's no valve train above this combustion chamber. No cooling fins (and the radiator visible to the upper left) assure you this one's water-cooled.*

*Another water-cooled, two stroke engine. The top center plug is a little more visible and you can see the radiator clearly.*

*The pipe side of a two stroke; notice the relative fatness and the varying diameter.*

There are two types of gasoline-powered, internal combustion engines used: four stroke and two stroke. A four stroke fires the spark plug and does the gasoline big bang every other time the piston "strokes" from the bottom to the top of the cylinder, so there are four strokes in a complete cycle. The other strokes are when a fresh fuel charge is drawn in (down stroke), compressed (up stroke), fired (down stroke) and exhausted (up stroke). A two stroke fires every time the piston comes to the top of the cylinder; exhaust, intake and compression are accomplished within the two strokes. Here are the key differences from a dirt bike rider's perspective:

- Four strokes have valves and cams (the valve train). We call 'em "thumpers" for the deep pulsing sound they make while running.
- Two strokes don't have valves and cams, but modern ones have a "power valve" and "reeds."
- A four stroke uses its valves to control a passageway from the carburetor to the cylinder for a fresh fuel-air charge and a different passageway for the hot post-combustion gases to exit via the exhaust pipe. The valves are timed by the cam which moves them, while the cam is timed to the up/down movement of the piston.
- A two stroke uses the reed valve, located between the carburetor and the cylinder, to help the piston be more efficient as it pulls each air-fuel charge into the cylinder, trapping the charge as the piston starts to move down. The power valve is used to change the position or size of the exhaust ports. The up-down movement of the piston creates a vacuum within the cycle to pull air-fuel into the bottom end of the engine, under the piston, push it up into the top end of the cylinder, above the piston, via passageways called transfer ports and allow it to escape post-combustion out the exhaust. The timing is accomplished as the piston covers and uncovers transfer ports and exhaust ports at varying positions within the cylinder.
- Four strokes run on straight gas, two strokes must have oil mixed with their gas (some two strokes have a separate tank for the oil and a pump to inject it into the air-fuel mixture as it enters the cylinder).

- Two stroke engines have dominated the high performance side of the dirt bike market for three decades, taking only a few years after their introduction to accomplish that feat. They are compact, light weight and very powerful. 250cc engines make nearly 50hp, with broad, usable powerbands. These characteristics make them perfect for dirt bikes.
- Four stroke engines have been making a huge comeback. While advanced designs and materials have greatly lightened this design and improved their power characteristics, it is the Environmental Protection Agency (EPA) that is forcing this "resurgence." The two stroke engine cannot be made to run clean enough without severe cost and performance impacts, so the dirt bike companies have put their R&D bucks into the four strokes. Just to be clear, it still takes the original competition rules adjustments, where almost twice as large of a thumper is allowed to race in the two stroke size classifications, to even the playing field. Expect two stroke engines to be phased out, starting with the manufacturers discontinuing R&D, as the EPA rules took effect in 2006. When allowed to compete with much smaller two stroke engines, so as to even out peak horsepower, the four stroke's longer powerband makes them easier to ride faster, longer. Of course, the idiocy of worrying about the pollution generated by dirt bikes is clear; one 747 flight lays out more than all the bikes in your state operated all year.

Dirt bike riders talk about "powerband" when they describe how an engine works for them. Powerband is a description of the usable power an engine makes vs. how fast it is spinning (rpms). As a basic rule, the slower an engine spins, the less power it makes and vice versa. We care because we want the small size and weight of a single cylinder engine in order to have a light, nimble machine, but we also want rapid acceleration. Designing a single cylinder engine to provide rapid acceleration means that the power has to be concentrated in a relatively narrow band of engine speeds (rpms). Two stroke engines tend to make their power at high rpms, four strokes, until very recently, tended to make less peak horsepower, but have a bigger spread of power, which means more, much more, than a two stroke at low rpm.

We would say that a thumper has more "bottom end" while a two stroke is "peaky." The manufacturers are always offering variants and in the two stroke world the reeds and power valves and such have been applied to spread out powerbands across the revs. Designs and to some extent subsequent tuning can create "low end" powerbands. Modern four strokes, given the allowed displacement offsets, make as much or more peak power and offer very wide powerbands.

Further, we can break down performance within the powerband. A bike might be described as "soft on the bottom, picks up in the low-mid, hits hard in the midrange and pulls hard all the way to a screaming top end." Or "pulls hard right off the bottom, has a monster mid and signs off early on top." Most modern engines tend to work well in most riding situations, but powerband characteristics do have an impact. Trail, slick and technical (tricky, slow) terrain is better ridden with a low-end powerband that trades maximum possible acceleration for traction (which yields more net acceleration in those conditions). Other types of riding favor top-end engines. In general, a beginning rider will do better with softer, low-end power, while a pro can handle explosive, top-end engines.

Engine sizes for dirt bikes range from 50 – 650cc. There are fairly distinct groupings based on competition classes, designed and named around two stroke engine sizes. Based on an engine generally being "no bigger than," these are: 50, 65, 80/85, 125, 250 and 500cc (two stroke sizes, the 250cc four stroke correlates with the 125cc two stroke, the 400-450 four stroke with the 250 two stroke. 500cc two stroke designs haven't been updated in a decade, partially because no human can handle any more power, partially because the market for them is small and partially because they're being supplanted by the modern big thumpers.

The modern four strokes began their comeback with 400cc designs, now typically 450cc, which are allowed in the 250cc "two stroke" class. Now the manufacturers are working on the 125cc class, which allows 250cc thumpers. It appears that the four strokes dominate this matchup and one manufacturer has stopped importing their two stroke 125. There are even 150cc thumpers that have hit the market to compete with the 85cc two strokes.

The non-competitive market is supported by an array of engine sizes. On the small end, they are intended to ensure an available progression of machines to set the offspring on as they grow up.

For the big kids, there are several specialty sizes. First, in the two stroke design, 200cc bikes offer a bridge between the ultra light and nimble 125s, with power more like a 250. The 300cc size likewise attempts to blend the all-around capabilities of a 250 with the oomph of a big bore. Special thumper sizes hit the big end between 500 and 650ccs.

There is also an intense sub-culture around incredibly customized, very expensive, what we used to call pit bikes – something to cruise to the rider's meeting on, visit friends, scope out different view spots around the track to check out lines, 50cc four stroke bikes. After building those little mills out to their reliability limit and beyond, they have expanded up into the 100 and 125cc four strokes. Of course, they're a blast.

## Frame

If the engine is the heart of the bike, the frame is the skeleton. The central, strongest component of the frame is called the backbone. Frames encircle or hold the engine and provide attachment points for the suspension and wheels, as well as the bodywork, seat, footpegs and a bunch of other parts and systems. Critical frame factors include strength and rigidity. The frame has to be strong enough to keep the engine and wheels aligned against the effects of the engine's

twisting power and the impacts of hitting uneven terrain. But it can't be too rigid, or too much shock will be transferred to the rider. If this happens, the frame will tend to act like a spring under certain impacts and loads. When it releases that energy, it will kick the whole bike in undesirable ways.

Most frames are made of round steel tubing, although there are full aluminum designs on more and more bikes.

## Transmission

Called the "tranny." An integral part of the engine assembly, dirt bike trannies are rugged, constant mesh, drum-shifted designs. They have four to six forward gears, generally more on the smaller engines, fewer on the larger – more gear ratios are needed to cover the more narrow powerbands in smaller engines.

Constant mesh means all of the pairs of gears are constantly engaged. Shifting means selecting which sets of gears are attached to the output shaft (which ends at the gear on the outside of the engine that the drive chain goes around, as opposed to the input shaft, which has all the gears always attached). The input shaft is spun by the crankshaft via the clutch. This was the obvious solution in achieving small and light, easy-shifting trannies operating under heavy engine loads and terrain impacts.

Selected gears are connected to the shaft by "dogs" that are keyed to the output shaft and can slide along it and have big rounded teeth on their sides which engage slots on the sides of the gears. The dogs are moved along the shaft by "shift forks" that look like the letter 'Y.' The top of the Y is connected to the dogs, pushing on both sides so as to move it smoothly along the shaft. The tail end of the Y rests in grooves in the "drum" which is a cylinder. The grooves go straight around the cylinder except in the cylinder positions corresponding to where the dog needs to move sideways to engage the correct gear, so the grooves then move angularly along the length of the cylinder. The cylinder is turned by the action of the shift lever. Moving the shifter up or down slightly turns the shift shaft, which is connected to the drum by a partial gear set. The drum is held in each gear position by a detent system.

All motorcycle transmission shift patterns have been standardized internationally for decades. We may not all drive on the same side of the road yet, but thank goodness we all shift on the same side of the bike. The shifter is on the left side of the engine, operated with the left foot. Pushing down achieves a downshift, lifting up an upshift. You cannot shift past first to sixth, or vice versa and neutral is located, as a gentle "half shift," between first and second. You might imagine the confusion and occasional terror, of moving between bikes which might shift on either side, in different patterns. Old timers can always relate a tale about shifting to the wrong gear, or miscounting and shifting past sixth, to first, blowing up the engine and landing on their head.

There have been automatic transmissions on dirt bikes; they have worked but have not caught on with the general market for a variety of reasons, including reliability. But don't count the engineers out. As material science progresses, they'll get the stuff they need to pull off the ultimate automatic dirt bike tranny. There are functional 2WD systems being refined, too.

Very small, generally 50cc bikes for very young beginners, sometimes have one gear only, there is no shifting.

## Clutch

The clutch's job is to allow you to separate the spinning engine from the tranny and thus disconnect the rear wheel. There are basic reasons for this, such as allowing the rider to shift out of neutral and into gear, controlling when the engine's power is to be connected to the tranny and thus the rear wheel. It allows for easy shifting between gears. The specialized design of a dirt bike clutch also allows the rider to actively modulate how much of the engine's power is passed through to the rear wheels, which is extremely useful. This simply means that it is okay to slip these clutches, a lot even, without hurting them (you can overdo it, of course).

The clutch, which is located on the right side of nearly all dirt bike engines, uses numerous alternating plates (both "drive," connected to the crankshaft and "driven," connected to the tranny's input shaft), to absorb the abuse and heat generated by slipping while also providing solid engagement at full release.

Dirt bike clutches are operated by a lever, always found on the left side of the handlebars. Squeezing the lever actuates the clutch (opens it, spreading the drive and driven plates apart) via a cable or a hydraulic system.

Recently emerging are automatic or slipper clutch designs, which involve replacing some of the drive and driven plates within the clutch. These came from the pavement racers and were first intended to automatically disconnect the tranny from the engine under rapid deacceleration which, due to engine braking, resulted in skidding and rear wheel hop on the asphalt. The other variant actually acts as an automatic clutch, with moving balls which respond according to engine and rear wheel rpm. Riders seem to love them or hate them. They are a bit expensive and not something you need to worry about at this stage of your riding career. Additionally, you can't bump start your bike with some of them.

Smaller bore 50-90cc bikes intended for young beginners are built with an automatic clutch, which simply operates according to engine rpm. Once the engine begins to spin faster than a pre-set rpm, it is solidly engaged. Movement of the shift lever forces a disengagement.

## Brakes

Dirt bikes have brakes on both wheels, except for those crazy speedway bikes, which have none. The stronger "disk" type are most common, but the older "drum" types are still used on smaller or less powerful bikes where they are certainly up to the task. The front wheel brake is always operated by a lever on the right side of the handlebars, the rear by a pedal on the right side of the engine, pressed on by the right foot.

*A rear drum brake. Notice the actuating rod.*

*Two examples of front drum brakes. You can see the actuating cables.*

Drum brakes use a cam to expand the position of the end of a set of brake "shoes" that form a circle just inside the metal cylinder inside the center of the wheel, called the hub. Squeezing the lever or pressing the pedal moves a cable or rod attached to a lever which turns the cam, which in turn "spreads" apart one or both ends of both brake shoes, effectively increasing the diameter of the circle they form, pressing them against the hub, accomplishing braking.

*A front disk brake. The shiny rotor gives it away. The caliper is tucked safely behind the fork leg.*

*A rear disk brake. Designing the caliper to be inside and above the swingarm offers it some protection, too.*

Disc brakes use hydraulic systems to squeeze brake pads against either side of a flat metal disk (called the rotor), which is attached to the wheel's hub. Disc brakes are much more powerful than drum brakes. They are more efficient at transforming the force applied by the rider at the lever or pedal into pressure between the pads and the braking surface. When disk systems first made it to dirt bikes, thcy tcndcd to bc uscd at the front wheel, where about 80% of the potential stopping effect is. Disc brakes are less affected by water, which is squeezed off during braking and dissipate the heat of braking quicker. Disc brakes, though, with their external rotor, are more prone to crash damage and some sort of guard is usually standard on at least the front wheel. Many riders add one to the rear and/or beef up the one on the front with an aftermarket part.

## Suspension

Riding a dirt bike over uneven ground, hitting roots and rocks, and jumping would not be any fun without suspension to absorb the impacts and shocks. Sure enough, the basic component of suspension is called a shock absorber. We call that part of the rear suspension the "shock". The front suspension with two "shocks," one on either side of the wheel for rigidity, we call "forks" even though it only looks like one fork.

Suspension systems generally use springs (one per each rear shock, one each per fork leg), to provide, well, suspension. The bike is held up, suspension fully extended, by the springs. When the wheels hit something, or the bike lands from a jump, the springs absorb the impact.

That would only create a pogo stick though and our bikes would bounce all over the place and be uncontrollable. So suspension systems have "dampening."

Dampening is intended to control how fast a suspension compresses or extends. This is called compression and rebound dampening. This is accomplished hydraulically, where special light oils are forced through complicated orifices as the suspension component compresses or rebounds. Intricate valving designs create dampening rates which vary automatically depending on the speed and magnitude of suspension movement, providing incredible suspension control and performance.

On modern bikes, both compression and rebound dampening rates are adjustable. Savvy riders will fine tune their suspension for the terrain and type of riding to be done that day. Many pro racers spend more time perfecting their suspension than they do tuning any other part of their bike.

*Regular forks used to be the norm. The smaller diameter tubes are bolted to the bike, while the larger diameter part, which moves over the skinny part as they slide up and down, is attached to the wheel. Notice the protective boot over the skinny part. This is to keep dirt away from the seal between the smaller and larger parts. The seal is to keep the fork oil in. Fork oil is the medium used to define dampening as it is forced through orifices during fork movement.*

*Upside down forks (now the norm). The large diameter part is attached to the bike, the smaller diameter to the wheel. The seal between them "faces" downward and is not so susceptible to dirt, but the lower legs are more exposed to roost and rock damage and a nick would tear at the seal, so there are plastic guards to protect them.*

There are two styles of forks common today, regular and upside down. Forks can change in length as their internal spring absorbs impact because they are basically made of two sections of pipe, one smaller so it is able to slide into the other. The smaller pipe is a very rigid piece of steel tubing; the other piece is typically aluminum. In regular forks, the inner steel piece is clamped to frame pieces called triple clamps (which connect to the main frame across the steering stem, around which the front end pivots or steers). The wheel and hub are attached to the aluminum parts of the forks, the part that moves up and down over the steel, clamped part. These are called sliders.

In upside down forks, the steel and aluminum pieces are swapped. This may have been nothing more than a marketing plot at first, but it did create a more rigid front end. The whole world of dirt bike frame and suspension design is one of tradeoffs between rigidity and flex. When upside down forks first appeared, some loved the rigidity, some lamented the loss of flex. They are now pretty much standard on high performance and racing dirt bikes.

Rear suspensions on dirt bikes use a swingarm, a u-shaped structure which cradles the rear wheel. The swingarm pivots around a large swingarm bolt, allowing the rear wheel to move up and down. In the typical single shock design, the shock is mounted vertically in front of the wheel and controls the movement of the swingarm. If there are two shocks, one is mounted on either side of the wheel. Most single shock designs use linkages to connect to the swingarm. These create different leverage ratios (progressively) between the swingarm and the shock across the range of swingarm pivoting, which helps designers produce a rear suspension that can be supple over small bumps and stiffer on the big hits.

*This view of a '74 Kawasaki KE100 shows a standard twin shock setup, one on either side of the rear wheel and swingarm.*

*On this much more modern '02 Kawasaki KX100, the single rear shock can be seen nestled within the forward section of the swingarm, in front of the rear wheel. There are also single shock designs where the suspender is mounted to one side of the swingarm only.*

## Chain/Sprockets

All dirt bikes transfer power from the engine/tranny to the rear wheel via a chain. The chain runs over a pair of "sprockets" (gears), a smaller one at the engine (at the tranny's output shaft) and a larger one at the rear wheel. The ratio, or number of teeth at one or both of these sprockets, can be changed with different parts to optimize performance for the conditions. Adding teeth to the rear or fewer teeth on the front increases the ratio, increasing acceleration rate but lowering top speed and the speed spread across each gear. Adding teeth to the front sprocket or removing them from the rear "raises" the gearing, slowing acceleration while increasing top speed. There is a basic relationship estimate of a change of three teeth on the rear being equivalent to one on the front for dirt bikes. Going too small, generally 12 teeth or less, on the front, tends to shorten chain life by bending it around a tight arc; going too big can cause clearance issues. Rear sprocket size range is less restricted; only too big might be a problem. In general, bikes are delivered with pretty spot-on gearing, such that useful changes are fairly small in scope.

There are two types of chain, standard and o-ring. Standard chain is just chain. It must be carefully cleaned and lubricated to survive for long on a dirt bike. O-ring chains use, brace yourself, o-rings (tiny rubber donuts), to seal grease in the working insides of the chain. Both can be used, as there is another trade-off between them - an o-ring chain absorbs a bit of engine power due to its greater internal friction caused by the seals. In general, an o-ring chain is used in muddy or wet conditions, a standard otherwise. The power difference is so slight compared to total available power that many simply run the o-ring version. O-ring chains tend to outlast standard chains, because the o-ring chains are always lubricated even when dirty, while standard chains vary from freshly cleaned and lubed to dirty and dry.

*A shot of the chain and the front sprocket, which is at the engine.*

*Here's a rear sprocket and chain, attached to the rear wheel.*

## Wheels/Tires/Spokes

Dirt bike wheels are light weight wonders. The tiny hubs are made of aluminum, as are the rims (there are some steel rims on lower-end models). The two are connected by spokes, which are strong and rigid, but do flex. You'll see cast wheels on street bikes, but they haven't satisfied dirt bike riders.

Spokes are the metal rods between the hub and wheel. We say that a wheel is laced up when it is assembled by installing the spokes. They are installed in a pattern where they crisscross and form triangles, which creates an intensely strong assembly that also provides lots of flex. Considering the huge pounding the wheels on a dirt bike must endure, this combination of strength and flex is a must. Spokes are adjustable, doing so is called truing a wheel. This is nothing more than ensuring that the wheel stays in a plane as it rotates, that it is round and there is no side-to-side wobble as it spins. It will be a rare day when you encounter a wheel that needs to be trued.

You *will* encounter loose spokes, especially during the first few hours of riding a brand new bike. Each spoke has two parts, the spoke/metal rod and the nipple. Always use the correct size spoke wrench, you'll quickly destroy the nipples if you try to use pliers or an adjustable wrench. The nipples are located at the rim end of the spokes and are simply a threaded connection that allows the spoke to be pulled tight between the hub and wheel. On the rear wheel, you'll notice that the spokes on either side of the rim lock tend to loosen up first.

If you are prepping a bike to be super reliable in rugged conditions, safety wire each point where the spokes cross. Some racing organizations still require this, even though wheel assemblies are much stronger than in years past. This will also help prevent a broken spoke from wreaking further havoc. The loss of one spoke in a wheel is not the end of your day, but if you lose a few, you'd better baby her home, because the problem is going to spread on a wheel so compromised. Replacement is easy once the tire is off.

Simply thread the new spoke from the hub to the wheel and connect with the nipple.

The majority of dirt bike riders use special dirt tires called "knobbies." Large, tall and widely-spaced rubber blocks designed to dig deep into the dirt make up the surface of knobbies. There is quite an array of knobby choices with tread patterns and rubber compounds designed for everything from soft sand and mud to hard packed, rocky terrain. There are specialized tread designs for trials bikes, flat track machines and dual sports.

Tires are arguably the most important performance feature of a dirt bike. The dirt we ride on would just as soon fly out of the way than stay put and provide traction for us to drive against. The performance difference between worn and fresh knobbies is astounding and experienced racers can feel the difference in acceleration, braking and cornering on even moderately worn skins. The wear starts as a rounding of the edges of the knobs, followed by loss of height. Pay attention to what brands and models other riders are using in the places where you ride and get a set as soon as whatever came on your bike shows significant wear.

Unless you can afford lots of tires, you may have to make a compromise between tire design purpose and tire life. For example, if your riding zone is a combination of loose soil like sand and rocky ground, you'll find a soft terrain design quickly chewing itself to pieces on the rocks. You'll have to compromise with a more intermediate terrain design, unless you always want to tip-toe through the rocks, but that is not why you went riding - is it?

One last part of the wheel you need to know about is the rim lock. In order to gain the traction we need in the dirt, we run quite low tire pressures, 12 psi being the common starting point. Tubeless tires won't work; there is not enough pressure to keep the bead, or edge, of the tire seated against the wheel, so tubes are a must to have a chance of staying inflated. With the low pressure, the forces of acceleration and braking are constantly trying to spin the tire relative to the wheel and they would quickly succeed without the rim lock. The valve stem would be ripped out of the tube – instant flat.

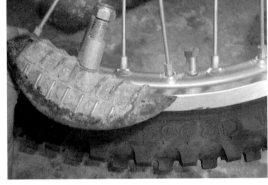

*The rim lock above locks the tire to the rim by tightening the nut.*

The rim lock is a simple clamp that locks the tire to the wheel. Look around the rear wheel of your dirt bike, you'll find the valve stem where you add air and another bolt with a nut on it sticking out - that is the rim lock. Inside the wheel is a rubber covered piece of metal shaped so that as the nut is tightened it pulls this against the tire and pins it to the wheel. All dirt bikes use at least one rim lock at the rear, most have one on the front and some have two on the rear.

We should cover one more item in the wheel assembly and that is the tube. There are three types - regular, heavy duty and the insert. A heavy duty tube is simply a thicker tube and a few extra bucks for one is generally a wise choice. Racers and long distance riders who simply must avoid flats go with an insert - this is an airless, solid rubber tube that takes a liberal application of grease and knuckle skin to install.

## Radiators

Most modern two stroke and four stroke engines are water-cooled. This allows the designers to keep engine temperatures consistent, or at least within a tighter range vs. air cooling. Considering the effect of temperature on the size of a metal part such as the piston, this means the designers can make the tolerances, or gaps between moving parts, tighter without normal expansion resulting in a "seizure," or turning the engine into "one piece." The radiators, made of aluminum to save weight, are located on both sides of the bike in front of and above the engine, basically between your knees as you sit on the bike. A water pump, located inside the right side of the engine and driven by the crankshaft, circulates coolant throughout the system. There is a cap on top of one of the radiators for checking and adding coolant. Note: As the radiators are aluminum, they can get crushed or punctured in a crash. Don't remove the plastic guards unless you replace them with tougher ones; not only do they protect the radiator, they also limit the cooling air at high speeds so the engine doesn't get too cold. When you realize repairing or replacing radiators can cost hundreds of bucks, guards suddenly seem like a good investment.

*The dirt bike radiator is behind the plastic guard. Except for some 80cc bikes which would only have one mounted to either side, and a few early water-cooled designs which placed one in the center, all bikes have two, one on each side.*

## Fuel Tank

Dirt bikes burn gasoline - the same as in your car - in their engines. In general the highest grade (premium) is used in all two strokes. Some thumpers run fine on lower grades. Very highly-tuned racing engines sometimes require specialized fuel called race gas. Aviation gas or jet fuel is totally inappropriate for dirt bikes. It is engineered for that special purpose and its characteristics when ignited in your cylinder are all wrong for what your engine needs. On most dirt bikes the fuel tank is located in front of the seat above the engine. The tank cap is vented so that fuel will flow freely down a hose into the carburetor via gravity. There is a valve called a petcock where the fuel flows out of the tank to allow shutting off fuel flow, or to access a small reserve amount of fuel in the tank.

## Carburetor

The carb takes fuel from the tank and mixes it with air that the piston sucks into the engine with each engine revolution. A choke is provided to add extra gas to the mixture to aid cold starting. Dirt bike carbs are very tunable via "jets" that provide different size holes for the fuel to be drawn through. "Rich" refers to having too much fuel for a particular throttle setting range and would be tuned by using a smaller jet. "Lean" refers to having too little fuel. A rich engine is not making maximum power. A lean engine will seem like it is tuned to maximum power, except that it is running too hot and will probably fail.

Except for a few '70s rotary valve engines, you'll easily spot the carb. It is just to the rear of the cylinder on every dirt bike. Rotary valve engines placed the carb on the right side of the engine, alongside the crankshaft. Now pay attention... a plate with a pie piece missing timed an opening between the bottom end of the engine and the carb, so that as the piston was going up (vacuum underneath) the air fuel charge would be sucked in. At top dead center the plate was "closed" and the downward motion of the piston (driven by the explosion of the previous air-fuel charge or the kickstarter) would pump the charge to the top of the cylinder above the piston via transfer ports, simply passageways in the sides of the cylinder between the bottom and top ends. Bringing the air-fuel charge in under the engine and pumping it to the top is called case induction - it is the norm on most modern two strokes, accomplishing it with a reed valve instead of a rotary valve. In a case induction engine more power is typical. In essence, separating the task of bringing a fresh air-fuel charge into the engine from the job of getting the exploded one out is more efficient and a bit of a form of supercharging (increasing the relative pressure of the charge) certainly helps. A reed valve is a simple set of flaps between the carb and the cylinder. When the piston is going up on a case induction engine they are forced open by the vacuum and air flows through the carb. As soon as the piston stops moving up at top dead center and heads down, the change in air pressure at the reeds allows them to return to their normally closed position and trap the charge in the engine. The piston moving down and adding pressure to the charge only forces the reeds more tightly shut.

## Air Cleaner

Often operated in extremely dusty conditions, dirt bikes require very efficient air filtration systems for their engines. The air cleaner is typically located in an enclosure under the seat, behind the engine. The enclosure is intended to protect the filter from raw dust and mud. The filter element is usually a foam construction supported by an open cage which can be cleaned and reused.

*The air cleaner consists of an air box and a filter inside. The box is the first defense against dirt and water, but a poor one, because it still has to freely admit air (usually from under the seat) for the engine to breathe. The foam filter is the final line of defense to keep crud out of your engine.*

## Exhaust/Silencer/Spark Arrestor

The exhaust system on a dirt bike is generally called the pipe. It connects to the engine at the front via a header pipe and runs all the way to the rear of the bike, with its exit on either side of the rear fender. The routing of the pipe is generally up and high along the side of the bike to keep it out of harms way – away from your leg, for example. There are heat shields where a rider might come in contact during normal riding situations.

At the exit end of the pipe there must be a silencer – unmuffled pipes are very loud. Except for bikes operated on private, closed courses, a spark arrestor must be added to or be an integral part of the silencer. Various designs exist to ensure that no hot sparks blow out of the exhaust and start a fire. Silencers use chambers, baffling (holes) and "packing," generally a fiberglass matting, to muffle sound (hey, that explosion is loud).

*The metal canister on the end of the pipe is the silencer and it may provide the spark arrestor function.*

There are two basic types of spark arrestors – screens and centrifugal. The screen method is obvious. The centrifugal method uses vanes to force the exhaust gases to spin, and any glowing particles are spun out into a catch area within the silencer. The issue with the screen type is that they eventually plug up, usually only on two stroke engines. I have personally struggled to get what was a perfectly running bike to start, checking the carb, changing the plug, pushing, towing, cussing, etc., until I removed a bolt-on screen type arrestor, wherein the bike started with one kick. A little work with an ice pick saved the day; otherwise they are cleaned and cleared with a torch and a wire brush. The centrifugal type needs no maintenance.

*The authorities will verify that you have a spark arrestor by poking a stick or wire into your exhaust outlet. Try not to wince. If the stick does not encounter a blockage, the tester will conclude that you do not have a spark arrestor.*

A thumper's pipe will be a generally simple tube with relatively the same diameter from the engine to the silencer. Two stroke pipes are much more complicated in design. After a section of constant diameter pipe right out of the engine, the diameter is increased to a wide belly section and then decreased back down to an exit section just before the silencer, called the stinger. Pay attention: the fat section in the middle and the "cones" at either end of it are intended to both help draw the exhaust gas out of the cylinder, making room for the next air/fuel charge and to reflect the pressure wave from a given explosion in the cylinder back to the cylinder/exhaust port just as the next air/fuel charge has arrived in the cylinder, to help hold it in. The rate of change of pipe diameter and the diameter and length of the fat section are tunable by pipe designers to change where and for how long in and over the rpm range that this expansion-extraction and pressure wave reflection system is working. The shape and tuning of a two stroke's pipe led to the original name of "expansion chamber" and the relation of chamber tuning to rpm led to the phrase "coming on the pipe," or the point in an engine's increasing rpm scenario where response shifts from somewhat lethargic to rip-snorting.

*A clear shot of the simplicity of a four stroke engine's exhaust pipe*

*A two stroke engine's pipe, with its fat belly and cones connecting it to the generally constant diameter tubes coming out of the engine and from the belly to the silencer.*

*A two stroke pipe with a guard mounted. Notice the "tuning dent" just above the guard.*

Aftermarket companies provide specialized pipes for almost all bikes. In many cases they can provide a performance increase over the stock pipe, although that is mostly a minor improvement in recent years and is only applied by a rider looking for every last little bit of power or by a simple replacement need due to crash damage. Aftermarket pipes are just as often purchased in order to change the power characteristics of an engine, such as to get more low or top end or to spread out the powerband of a peaky engine.

Two stroke pipes, because of their wide belly and very specific requirements for the length of each section, are much harder to protect and special guards are commonly added by their owners.

## Fenders/Bodywork

The fenders exist solely as a place to cover with dirt bike stickers. Just kidding, they sometimes perform a secondary function— keeping away the rocks, mud and dirt your tires would otherwise spray you and the rest of the machine with.

Number plates: The front number plate, located across the forks above the front fender, has a primary purpose of being a place to mount - drum roll here - your number. It also serves as a guide to keep your front brake cable from snagging on the handlebar mounts or the top of the forks. With a cable-operated front brake, this was always good for a solid crash. In nighttime events such as an overnight enduro, the front number plate may also carry a headlight.

The side number plates: Like the front they are intended for numbers. Even riders who never have or will enter a race tend to mount their favorite number. Two schools of thought on number selection (assuming you aren't actually racing in an organization that assigns numbers) seem to be either your personal, lucky number or the number your favorite professional racer is assigned. Any number – in repeated actual scientific tests – makes you faster. The side number plates are also useful in helping keep your feet away from the rear wheel.

Radiator wings. These are only found on water-cooled bikes. These serve several purposes. They tie the outboard edges of the radiators to the tank with triangulation (resulting in strength), they direct air flow into the radiators and provide smoothly transitioning bodywork for your knees to grip. Of course, they are another excellent place for stickers!

## Controls

This section is intended to get you familiar with the things you need to operate correctly in order to ride your bike.

### Petcock

Now here's an ancient term that has hung on through all the years that there have been motorcycles. It is shorter than fuel tank valve and certainly adds character when blended into your dirt bike tales. Your bike won't run for long if you fail to set your petcock to "on" (or "run," depending on your bike). You'll find yours somewhere under the fuel tank. They're almost always metal and have a small handle used to turn them. You need to turn it from off to on, and not to reserve until you have already run out of gas.

*Four styles of petcocks. They are always at or very near the bottom or low point of the fuel tank, have a lever to change them from Off to On or if available, Reserve, and tubing from their outlet down to the carb. Note: some newer designs are fuel injected and do not have a petcock.*

So petcocks have two (on/off) or three (plus reserve) positions you can turn them to. How do you know where to turn it? Well, as if the owner's manual might actually help, some have "ON," "OFF" and if available, "RES," printed on the petcock's face plate behind the little handle. Sometimes you aim the pointer on the handle at the word, sometimes you place the tail of the handle over the word. Clearly, like the shifter and shift pattern, it would help to standardize petcock operation. Until then, you are either going to figure it out, someone is going to tell you, or the owners manual will actually make it clear. There is another way. Ensure that you actually have gas in the tank. Follow the fuel line from the petcock to the carburetor. Decide which end of the tubing would be easiest to remove and take it off. There is probably a simple little reusable clamp around the tubing. If you can, remove it from the carb end and place the open line into a small can to catch any gas that runs out. If gas starts flowing as you remove the tubing, the petcock is set to ON or RES. Turn the petcock to its different positions; the fuel flow or lack of it will show you the on-off part. Clean up the gas you've spilled.

The Reserve fuel system is a simple design. The part of the petcock which sticks up into the fuel tank has two inlets, one at the end of a tall tube. When the gas level falls below the top of the tube, the ON position will no longer flow fuel. Moving the petcock to RES lets gas flow through the lower inlet. Reserve usually offers only a small amount of gas, approximately half a gallon, just enough for an emergency run back to the truck.

Every dirt biker has forgotten to turn their petcock on at the beginning of a ride or race. A bike will run for a while off the fuel in the carburetor - just down the trail before going dry is embarrassing, but running dry after getting the start of your life and leading a race will have you banging your head against your truck.

Dirt bike range varies significantly. Tank size, riding style and type of terrain (speed) are key variables. For typical adult size two stroke and modern thumpers you'll find you get something between 25 and 45 miles to the tank. At the expense of some comfort there are aftermarket tanks available for many bikes that can double their range.

## Choke

Choking is what you'll want to do to your bike if you try to start it when it is cold and don't utilize the choke. The function of this device is simple, it richens the air/fuel charge (more fuel) which helps cold starting.

Chokes are operated by moving a lever or pulling a knob. Most are connected directly to the carb, some are mounted near the center of the handlebars and are connected to the carb's choke by a cable.

*Clockwise from the upper left, here are most of the types of chokes you'll encounter; the pull-up knob, the lever raised alongside the carb, the lever lifted out and away from the carb, the infamous "hidden" choke, the up-behind-the-front-number-plate knob and the pull-out knob. Not pictured includes; a*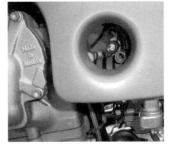

*tickler knob (pressed down to free flow gas from the tank to the engine, essentially bypassing the carb) and the tricky, raise the tiny skinny lever up, then pull it up and over a détente bump to get it to stay pointing straight up types.*

The lever type are usually pressed down to turn them on, the knob type require pulling or lifting the knob. Reverse direction to turn the choke off.

Dirt bike chokes do not provide a "cover" to the air inlet of the carb like most cars. Instead, they open up an alternate air path around the closed slide in the carb, as well as a tube from the air path to the fuel in the float bowl. Therefore, opening the throttle at all on a bike while the choke is on negates it being able to do its job.

## Kickstarter/Electric Starter

Most all bikes have a kickstarter located on the right side of the engine. You'll find a few on the left and the owners of such bikes always have an unassailable chain of logic proving that to be superior. The rest of us never buy it. They all fold in (out of the way for riding) and out (for starting), sometimes just the end section meant for your boot, sometimes the whole starter. Some brands thoughtfully have the words kickstarter embossed on them in big letters.

*The basic kickstarter, folded out away from its stowed position snuggled alongside the engine, with boot in place and ready to activate.*

*Several magic buttons. The starter is a small electric motor, usually behind but sometimes in front of the engine's cylinder.*

More and more bikes have electric start systems. We call the start switch the magic button. The ease of starting (especially when you stall in a dicey place, but also for dead engine start races) is off-set by the weight of the motor and the required battery.

## Footpegs

You'll find the footpegs sticking out of either side of the bike at the bottom/center of the frame near the rear of the engine. They can fold up and out of the way in a crash to keep them from breaking away from the frame and from breaking your leg. They're spring loaded to keep them in place otherwise. They are usually surfaced with a serrated edge to help keep your boots in place, while kid's bikes might have rubber-coated ones instead. A key part of controlling your bike happens at the boot-footpeg interface – more on this later.

## Handlebars

Connected to the front end of the motorcycle, on the top triple clamp, the handlebars are a key interface with your motorcycle, providing both steering and mounting for critical hand-actuated controls. We call them "bars" for short. The throttle, clutch lever and front brake lever are mounted on them, along with the engine kill switch and sometimes the choke lever. You'll steer your bike with them and use them to pull your weight forward and backwards relative to the bike as you ride over varied terrain.

Handlebars are made of steel or aluminum and a flex-rigidity trade-off is part of this equation. Aluminum bars are lighter and the controlled flex of recent designs is felt to reduce arm fatigue, but they are more expensive. Steel bars, if bent slightly, can be straightened.

At the ends of the handlebars are the grips, what you wrap your hands around. There is a huge array of different rubber compounds available, offering different "stickiness" or grip, diameters, colors and durability.

## Throttle

The throttle is always located on the right side of the bars. The throttle rotates on the bars, pulling a cable connected to the carb. A spring in the carb is always trying to close the throttle. The direction of rotation of the throttle to open it is to pull the top back towards you. From the right side of the bike, looking at the end of the throttle, the opening rotation is counter-clockwise.

The throttle's rotation is limited to around a quarter turn. It should always quickly return to close by itself – twist it to full and release it to verify that. If it does not, DO NOT ride the motorcycle until the problem is found and fixed. While it is fun to sit on a bike and work the levers and twist the throttle, keep your hands off your buddy's modern four stroke bike's throttle. Twisting them can make the bike extremely difficult to start, because an accelerator pump is activated and the engine will flood.

## Clutch Lever

The clutch is operated by a lever always found on the left side of the handlebars. The lever either uses a cable or hydraulics to transmit lever movement to the actual clutch.

## Brakes

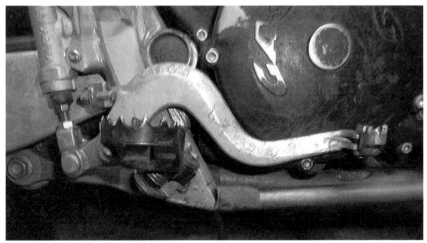

*A typical rear brake pedal.*

The front brake is controlled by a lever always located on the right side of the handlebars. For drum-style brakes, lever motion is transmitted to the front brake by a cable. For disc-style brakes, hydraulics are used. The rear brake is controlled by a pedal always found by the right foot peg. For drum-style brakes, pedal motion is transmitted by a rod, or in rare cases, a cable. For disc-style brakes, hydraulics are used.

## Shifter

In the early days, manufacturers used every possible design of foot-operated shift mechanism. Located on the right or left side, moving the lever up or down to shift to the next higher gear and with neutrals located in different places in the pattern, it was difficult to take your buddy's bike out for a spin. While riding a different brand could be dangerous, some designs were suicidal, like a rotary design where an accidental shift higher than the top gear brought you back around to first.

Fortunately, the needed standardization was widely accepted. Some manufacturers were delayed by design and tooling cycles and a few more obscure makes couldn't afford to adapt, which helped seal their fate in the market.

Shift lever location and operation were standardized to the left side, with downward movement of the lever shifting to a lower gear; up, a higher gear and neutral located between first and second. Further, attempting to shift lower than first or higher than top gear (most often fifth, but four and six speed gearboxes are more likely on big and small bore bikes, respectively) results in the shifter stopping firmly – a major improvement over a mis-shift blowing up your gearbox.

## Kill Switch

Pure dirt bikes don't have ignition or keys; there is nothing to turn on to enable the engine to run (other than the petcock, if you want it to keep running). So, such bikes need a way to turn the motor off, hence the kill switch. This is generally a button on the left side of the handlebars that when pressed, simply shorts the electricity that would have otherwise become the spark leaping across the gap in the plug.

*Find and know your kill switch. Here are four examples.*

Some dirt bikes, especially dual sports, have a regular keyed ignition, but they often have a form of a kill switch on the right side of the bars, usually a moveable arrow. Centered is on, up or down is off.

Enduro/off-road models usually have a control "box" with a switch for the lights, button for the horn and a kill switch.

It is important that you know where your kill switch is and how to operate it. The time will come when you want to stop the engine, NOW. As in, you've crashed and the throttle is stuck in the ground, wide open and you've got but a few seconds to shut her down before the engine self destructs.

In lieu of a kill switch, or one that doesn't function, you have two choices to get the motor to stop running. First and less desirable, turn off the petcock and let it run out of gas. This can take a couple of minutes and the engine might race (gain rpms significantly) as it goes lean. Second, put it in gear, jam on both brakes and ease the clutch out to kill it.

## Choosing A Bike

You live in one of the finest times in terms of the depth and breadth of the selection of dirt bikes you can choose from. True, we don't quite have the large number of unique manufacturers we did in the 70s, but the count has certainly increased over the last few years. What is impressive is the number of models available. There are bikes of every size, two and four stroke, for everyone from beginners to Pro racers. The manufacturers want you to be able to start with a selection of possibilities and then keep you on their brand no matter where your riding life takes you. Naturally, the biggest selection of models are aimed at the younger riders.

The following will help you think about which bike to purchase; new or used, engine, bike size and other special considerations.

### Intended Uses

Considering the age and desires of the intended rider, these rules of thumb will help you select the right bike.

For a beginner, tend toward small and slow. The less confident initially and/or more likely to have a more gradual learning curve, the more you will want to put a bike underneath that a rider can physically dominate. The rider should be able to stand up and completely clear the seat and the bike – they will naturally do this rather than personally hit that tree. The powerband characteristics should be soft and smooth, simply not capable of surprising or overwhelming the beginner with any hit. Small four stroke models fit this bill perfectly.

A young terror who is fearless on his bicycle and skateboard might be more able to handle a first bike that is bigger and/or more powerful. But again, you may still want to start with a soft motored bike. A key facet of learning is being able to control how quickly you challenge your envelope and a child hasn't learned that lesson.

Pay close attention to a fast learner's progress or you'll find the starter bike thrashed beyond decent re-sale quite suddenly. There are plenty of aggressive little mini-racer two strokes available.

If the new rider is focused on motocross, then bias that first bike towards that usage. If this racer is big enough for a full-sized bike, start them on a 125cc class bike first. Jumping straight to larger displacements seems to lead to sloppy technique, where a smaller engine demands more finesse.

If we're looking at a new trail rider, by all means get a trail-oriented bike. Don't handicap an off-roader with MX style, hard hitting powerbands mated to a suspension tuned to big jumps and whoops rather than plushed out for rocks and roots.

The majority of bikes end up being simply play ridden. A little two track or trail, a bunch of runs over a discovered jump, a hillclimb attack, some play racing, wheelie attempts, another donut, some cross country. For this kind of riding, guess what? An MX or a trail-oriented bike will do great!

## Air-cooled/Water-cooled

Simply put, that hot little engine is kept cool by either the air that flows over it as you ride, or by liquids with a radiator and a pump (yes, air flow through the radiator cools the water-cooled bike). It is pretty easy to instantly tell which is used on any bike.

In general, modern two and four stroke bikes are water-cooled. This system allows designers to keep engine temperatures within a tighter range. Tight thermal control means better control of the expansion of internal parts, which allows for tighter clearances and tolerances for pistons and rings providing better performance.

Air-cooled engines are obviously simpler, have no relatively delicate radiators and hoses to be protected, no coolant to check and are easier to do engine work on. You'll find them in bikes whose primary design goal is rugged reliability and general play riding and trail use.

You can overheat by running the engine with the bike stationary. With no air flow over an air-cooled cylinder or through the radiators, the systems can't do their job.

## New vs. Used?

I want exactly what I want! That bike! That new one!

The bottom line answer to this question starts with your bottom line. What can you afford? New full-size dirt bikes cost more. Used machines with decent life left in them will be less, but watch out for a sweetheart deal,.

A few other factors you might consider, not that they have the slightest chance of having an impact on your decision once you've fallen in love with a particular unit:

Is there a dealer nearby that carries parts or can service it?
Is this your first bike? If you're planning to upgrade after six months or it is for a fast growing youngster, it might be cheaper to start with a used one.
Will the bike be handed down through a brace of children? A new one might make it all the way.

## As a rule, for used bikes:
- Aftermarket parts add no value.
- The smaller the engine, the faster it wears out.
- A raced bike is not necessarily a bad purchase. Serious racers tend to take better care of the machine than the average play rider.
- The older the bike, replacement parts are more expensive and harder to obtain.
- Early models from manufacturers working to penetrate the North American market can be even harder to deal with than old bikes.
- Performance has gone through several significant phases over the decades:
- Single shock/linkage rear suspensions appeared in the early 80s and are almost always superior to twin shock designs.

- Power valve equipped engines appeared in the late 80s and always offer better overall power than those without.
- Disc brakes became standard by the early 90s. Drum brakes don't compare, although they are well suited to smaller, slower bikes.
- Frame designs improved significantly in the late 90s.

For most women, children and some men, a simple facet of a bike's suitability is the pick-up test. Begin by asking the salesperson if you can gently lay the bike on the showroom floor. The prospective buyer should be able to easily pick the bike up. If not, it's too big and too heavy and they will curse the bike the few times they ride it. Face it, the thing is going to end up on the ground.

Some folks will have no idea how to pick up a bike and would have trouble getting a bicycle off the ground. It's okay to show a prospective new owner how. First, turn the handlebars so that they are parallel to the ground. If the bike is lying on its left side, the bars will be turned as though the wheel is being turned to the right. Vice versa for the right side. Then, stand next to the seat, bend your legs all the way into a deep knee bend and grab the handlebars as though you were going to ride the bike. Squeeze the front brake lever to apply the brake. Next, leverage the bike up against its wheels by both pushing your legs to straighten them and leaning against the seat as it comes up off the ground. You can stop when the seat reaches your thigh to reposition your feet or your body, just keep that front brake on and lean into it. Complete standing the bike upright when you're ready.

**The Pick-Up Test**

*Can the rider get the bike off the ground by themselves? If barely able to, by the time they're tired from riding a bit, on about the third required hoist, they may no longer be capable.*

If you can't turn the bars out in the real world because the one end is stuck in the mud or drilled into the loam, lean against the bars rather than the seat as you lever the bike up with your body.

A rider lifting a bike up with decent technique, if testing a machine that is too heavy, will find that they can't get the thing off the ground much at all. If they can get it up to where the seat is at the thigh, about 45 degrees, it gets much easier after that.

Understandably, this test may not apply to a very young or new rider. You'll soon realize that you will never want junior riding very far away from you, unless you live for repeated 100 yard sprints to wherever it has been dropped next.

## The Kick Start Test

This is a little trickier, it can sometimes take a while to teach someone to kick start a bike. But there can be a gap between some bikes and some riders, where they just won't have the strength to ever reliably start it.

Again, the younger the new rider, the less this test applies. It's a second reason to keep a very young beginner within the distance you'll happily walk to.

## The Clutch Pull Test

This used to be a much more serious issue. I remember working tennis balls and hand exercisers so that I could take Dad's Benelli out. That thing took some serious pull. These days clutches are incredibly easy to operate, especially with hydraulically-operated designs. Still, there are bikes out there which have a clutch too tough for a given rider.

## Bounce It

A time honored tradition during the inspection of any bike, whether you're looking to buy or just checking out your buddy's ride, is the bounce test. Straddle the bike, grab the front brake and throw yourself against the bars, compressing the forks as hard as you can. Too soft or too hard and you'll know it. Now drop all your weight down on the seat and try to compress the rear suspension. Really, this is all mostly useless, but everybody does it. Don't fight it. For a used bike, this can expose loose or worn suspension parts. Look for oil weeping out of the fork seals.

## Other Used Bike Tests

As a beginner, buying a used bike almost demands that you find an experienced rider who also has dirt bike mechanical savvy to bring along on any inspection.

Get each wheel off the ground. By grabbing the top and bottom of the tire and attempting to twist it, you can detect worn axle bearings, worn swingarm bearings (rear) and worn steering bearings (front). Unless so bad that it is possible that hubs, the frame, or the swingarm are damaged, their condition is a bargaining chip, no more, no less.

Open the airbox. Is the filter spotless and oiled? If not, suspect poor maintenance. Encountering a bike for sale that isn't up-to-date on its maintenance or has not been cleaned spotless is a bike to walk away from, unless the price is ridiculously low. If the seller couldn't be inspired to clean and maintain it for sale, imagine how inspired they were when it wasn't for sale. Do a compression test if you can, that is your simplest motor wear inspection. While the plug is out, inspect it for apparent jetting accuracy. How much black mung appears to be drooling out the tail pipe is another jetting indicator on a two stroke machine.

The condition of other parts that wear out (tires, chain/sprockets, grips, brake pads), become another bargaining chip. Dented pipes, torn seats, shredded graphics? Bargaining chips. Estimate the cost of replacement and attempt to get the price lowered accordingly, if the seller hasn't already adjusted it down.

Ideally, you'll want to test a used bike when it is stone cold. Insist on it. You want to see how it starts cold and warms up, both for the data you may collect about its condition and to gain access to the current owner's personal knowledge. Warm the bike up fully. Does it idle? Smell the exhaust. If it is a two stroke and you think you detect burning gear oil, walk, no, run away. Ride it for at least 10 minutes. Go through all the gears many times testing the shifting with and without the clutch - upshifts only on the latter. Attempt to make the clutch slip by shifting to third going way too slowly. Then let the clutch out and pin it to test for slippage. The motor will clearly rev beyond the provided acceleration if the clutch is failing.

Always remember, if you crash, over-rev or otherwise cause a bike you are testing to break, you will either be paying to repair it or buying it as is.

If you buy a used bike from a private party, be sure to ask what brand of two stroke and gear oil has been used. Learn what maintenance has been done recently and ask for receipts. Ask what the owner would do next to the machine if they were going to keep it and plan on getting such done soon.

## When You Get Your Bike Home

Fight the temptation to just jump on it and ride the wheels off, if you can, and do the following first. Everything on the list applies to a new or a used bike. A dealer does forget things too.

- Change the gear oil (do this very soon for a new bike, right away for a used bike).
- Clean and oil the filter (used only).
- Inspect and replace the plug if needed (used only).
- Check ALL nuts and bolts, especially the handlebar clamps, the axles and front axle pinch bolts, the steering crown nut, the triple clamp-fork bolts, engine mounts, swingarm bolt/nut, silencer mount bolts and bodywork mounting bolts.
- Check the radiator coolant.
- Check tire pressure.
- Check the brakes (look at the shoes and/or pads for wear level).
- Check the spokes.

## The Dealer

New or used, you've got to have a dealer that carries or services your brand nearby. Your dealer can mean so much more. Advice, places to ride, events, hooking you up with other riders, your dealer can be a focal point for your pursuit of this sport. Strongly consider the relationship you think you can establish with the people at a potential dealership. Dealers reward good, repeat customers who are pleasant to deal with; you might get parts discounts, deals on new bikes, first shot at trade-ins and other benefits.

## Bike Progression Plans

Unless you must, try to avoid rare or troubled models; you'll pay come resale time. Always be planning ahead to your next bike. Never forget the first rule of dirt bike ownership and don't give up the bike you have until your hands are firmly around the grips of the next one.

As a beginner, plan on needing to move to your second bike within six to twelve months, perhaps sooner. Try to make that first bike a common, desirable model.

### Hand Them Down Through Your Family Plan

Within a family, it is easy to set up a progression of bikes, maximizing the value obtained from each purchase. This works as long as the offspring are going through early growth and generally learning about riding. If your tykes decide to race, you'll quickly find them each moving through individual machine progressions.

Another notion you might find valuable is brand commonality across your stable. There can be many common parts between the different sizes and displacements within a brand. This can lessen the amount of spares you feel the need to keep on hand, as well as be a ride saver when you discover too late to hit the shop, that something is broken.

# CHAPTER 4

## *GETTING OTHER STUFF YOU'LL NEED*

Just getting your bike and riding gear isn't enough. Unless you never ride anywhere but right out of the shop on your property, heck, even if that's all you do, you'll need most of the following stuff.

### Gas Can

No, that rusting little metal one gallon job for the lawnmower won't do. Sure, some bikes have enough range to satisfy you for a day, but no bike can do it for a weekend. And if you are riding 99% of the modern two stroke models, you'll need to be mixing oil with your gas. So, you need a gas can. The basic gas can you can find anywhere is made of plastic and commonly has a capacity of five gallons.

*Perhaps a color to match your bike?*

Remember, you get what you pay for. The best have the heaviest, thickest walls, yet are translucent enough to easily see how full they are. The bigger the spout, the faster the fill job. A separate vent, rather than integral with the fill tube, seems to smooth (stop surging) and increase flow. A filter in the neck is preferred; gas cans that spend a lot of time around dirt tend to get dirt in them. Clean gas is a key contributor to a happy, long living motor.

Off-road racers who often exceed even the extended range oversize aftermarket tanks offer seek to shave seconds off their pit stops by using "dry break" systems. Special cans mate with special tank spouts and with the pull of a trigger, dump gallons in a few seconds, filling the tank to the brim and separating without spilling a drop (usually), hence the name.

NEVER FORGET THIS. When you fill a plastic can with gas, always take the can out of your truck and place it on the ground. As it turns out, gasoline pouring out of that spout generates an electric charge, which can build up to a level where it can create a spark. Putting the can on the ground provides a way for the charge to dissipate.

## Two Stroke Oil - How to Mix

It is likely your two stroke motorcycle needs to have two stroke oil mixed with its gasoline, but a few use an oil pump drawing from a tank.

I'm not going to get into which oil to use. Your bike's manufacturer will certainly have a recommendation, as will everyone you ride with, magazine articles will have test results, yikes! There are two basic types, petroleum and synthetic (and some blends). A few tips, though. Do not jump around; pick an oil and stay with it (so pick one you can purchase reliably). Especially don't change between petroleum and synthetic. The change in the amount of oil in the gas may have a significant impact on your jetting. This tip really arose from the days when a synthetic was a "bean oil" and mixing it with a petroleum oil resulted in globules that wouldn't go through the carb's jets, thus causing expensive engine internals running lean and without oil to eat themselves. Don't use automatic transmission fluid. (Don't laugh. In an emergency, it will barely suffice.) Modern two stroke bike engines are highly-engineered machines and they need highly-engineered oils. Don't use cheapo, generic, two stroke oil if you want maximum power and reliability.

Typical petroleum oil ratios are in the 32 – 40:1 range. Full synthetics use 50 – 100:1 ratios, blends are usually around 50:1. You may still find some manufacturers recommend 20:1, but this has been largely discredited as too much oil. Not only does it tend to mung up the entire exhaust system, it interferes with the proper action of the piston rings.

Mixing is not hard to do! The key term is ratio. Riders will argue over running 32:1 vs. 40:1, or all the way up to 100:1 ratios suggested with some pure synthetics. The big number always represents the amount of gasoline, the small number's the amount of oil. Both numbers have to be in the same units of measure, typically fluid ounces. The smaller the gasoline number, the more oil there is in a given amount of gas.

You will need a gas can; mixing it clearly requires knowing exactly how much gas you are adding oil to. In a pinch you could add a specific amount of gas to your tank, pour in the correct amount of oil and shake it up. Most would only do this in an emergency, adding a whole number of gallons makes calculating the ratio much easier, so just how many gallons do you need to fill the tank, anyway?

We'll start with the simplest example, one gallon of gas. You need to know how many ounces that is in order to apply the ratio to determine how many ounces of oil to add. Follow this: there are eight ounces in a cup, two cups in a pint, two pints in a quart and four quarts in a gallon. So, (8 X 2 X 2 X 4=128) there are 128 ounces in a gallon. We'll go with a ratio of 32:1, which is common because it is on the safe side of gas-oil ratios (many manufacturers recommend it) and also because 32 conveniently divides evenly into 128. But I go too fast.

What the ratio means is that for every X amount of gasoline in ounces, one ounce of oil is added. So, if I have a gallon (or 128 ounces) of gas and I'm going to add one ounce of oil for every 32 ounces of gas, I need to know how many times 32 goes into 128. 128 divided by 32 equals 4. You would add four ounces of oil to one gallon of gas to achieve a 32:1 ratio.

Let's jump to five gallons and a ratio of 40:1. If one gallon is 128 ounces, five gallons is 640 ounces. Divide 640 by 40 and you get 16. It so happens that a typical bottle of oil holds 16 ounces, so it gets real easy, just dump it into a can with five gallons in it, voilà, 40:1!

If you don't happen to always use a ratio of 40:1 and five gallons, you are going to need a way to measure oil. Many oil cans provide a crude measurement window, pour out a bit, see where it lines up, repeat until you've just poured in a tad too much. Get a plastic measuring cup. Even better, your dealer has one that also includes markings for various ratios. The ratio side is not necessarily easy to use though. You have to be mathematical enough, for example, to know that 16:1 at 2.5 gallons is the same as 32:1 for five.

Remember, be precise and get the right ratio every time. You will become proficient at stopping the gas pump right at 5.0 gallons, but you will only be moderately accurate at measuring your oil to within a tenth of an ounce. The magnitude of your measuring error, as a percentage of the total amount of oil measured, will go down the greater the amount of oil measured. Simply stated, your error will be less if you mix for five gallons rather than one.

Don't get hung up on all this, though. A reasonable level of care in preparing your mix will get you close enough and your bike will be happy.

Okay, I promised, simple ratio math. Write your ratio (this example uses 40:1) and the amount of gasoline in ounces (for five gallons) like this, the "X" stands for how much oil you'll need:

$$\frac{1}{40} = \frac{x}{640}$$

Now, "cross multiply" and set those equal to each other:

$$40 \times x = 1 \times 640, \text{ or } 40x = 640$$

Now, divide both sides by 40, which leaves you with:

$$\frac{40x}{40} = \frac{640}{40} = x = 16 \text{ ounces of oil needed}$$

## Tools – Metric and Special Purpose

Dirt bikes use metric-sized fasteners. Your English wrenches won't work, except for a few exceptions where they match closely, like 9/16'' and 14mm. Typically you'll need wrenches and sockets in 8, 10, 12 (13, still, for most European brands), 14, 17 and 19. It is also likely that you will need metric Allen (properly called hex) wrenches, the socket drive units or "T" handle designs work best. Get a low pressure tire gauge, too, one that is accurate in the 5-20 psi range. A torque wrench is extremely valuable to have. I'll stop here, as a dirt bike owner you will soon own all sorts of tools you never dreamed existed, like exhaust spring pullers and spoke wrenches and custom ones to please any gear head.

*A selection of spoke wrenches.*

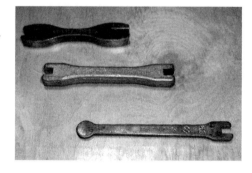

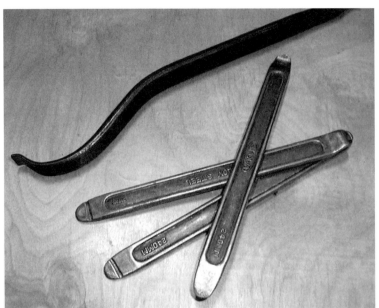

*The author's favorites. The three are simple, standard tire removal tools with one flat end and one slightly hooked end. Note the groove ground by the owner across the flat end, which is a useful "click" indicator to help prevent sticking the wrench too far into the bead-rim gap, as well as a secure pivot when leveraging the bead in or out. The long curved one works great for getting a new tire's first bead over the rim.*

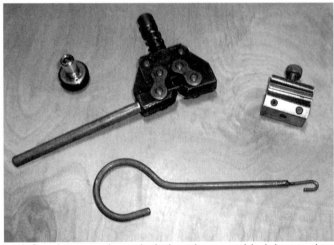

*From the top left, a jet wrench, a chain breaker, a cable luber and an exhaust spring puller. You can get by without them, but they make your job easier and they will puzzle your non-riding friends who happen to rummage through your tool box.*

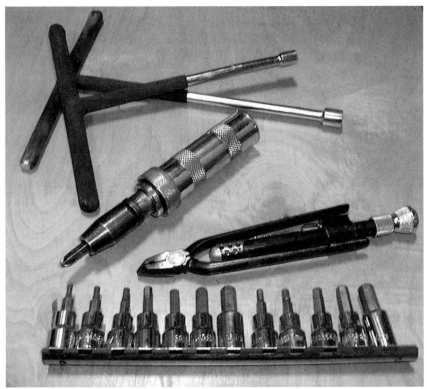

*Some more desirable tools. From the top, T-handles, an impact driver, wire wrap pliers and hex (Allen) socket wrenches*

*These are necessary specialty tools if you do much work yourself. From the left, inside snap ring pliers, a compression gage and outside snap ring pliers (okay, the latter can be switched to do either job)*

## Chain Lube

Get a can of chain lube. Realize that your dirt bike's chain is the most abused piece of metal on the machine, transmitting huge loads very rapidly, getting stretched and strained, while spinning itself through dust, mud, water and rocks. It is amazing that they survive at all. And they won't if you don't attempt to keep them clean and definitely keep them lubed. Do it every ride!

There are all sorts of old-time chain oiling methods. I too have heated gear oil gently in a pan on the stove and placed my cleaned chain in it to soak.

Instead, go with modern chain lube. It is engineered to penetrate yet stay put as your chain does its job. Note: there are two types of chain, regular and o-ring. O-rings technically need no lube, they are permanently lubed by the grease trapped behind the o-ring seals. But if you don't do something to your o-ring chain, it will look rusty shortly after you wash it. Many generously apply a light lubricating oil from a spray can. There are also specific o-ring chain lubes you can buy.

*Two shots intended to emphasize the correct application of any chain lube to the inside of the loop formed by the chain as it wraps around the sprockets.*

Apply chain lube to the inside of the loop formed by the chain. Put the bike up on a stand or a crate, aim the nozzle or tube of the can at the edge of the plates along the side of the chain and slowly spin the wheel as you apply the lube. Do both rows of plates, make sure you go at least once around. Spraying lube on the rollers in the center of the chain is a waste of lube, it goes nowhere useful and simply spins off. Continue to spin the tire for at least a dozen revolutions, the centrifugal force will drive the oil through and therefore into, the chain. If you don't have a stand to put the bike on, but have a kickstand, you can lean the bike up on the front wheel and the stand, but you'll need a buddy to spin the tire for you.

## Gear Oil

When you get a bike, find out what kind of gear oil it takes and buy it now. Get quality stuff designed for motorcycles, they take your clutch into account, as well as the stresses of the constant mesh transmission. You need to keep your gear oil fresh and depending on how hard you ride, you may need to change it every few hours. You will definitely want to change it after a few days of riding. Always having the correct oil on hand will encourage you, as soon as you do change it, to buy the next bottle.

Again, your dealer, your friends and the press will all be trying to convince you that their recommendation is best. And again, you need to choose between petroleum and synthetic oil. While I have used petroleum, synthetic and blended two stroke oil in my tank with good results all the way around, trannies seem to shift easier and last longer with synthetics.

## Filter Oil

Your dirt bike is equipped with an air filter. It will get dirty. Because it is made of foam, you can clean and reuse it. But the foam itself is only so effective; therefore, it needs to be coated throughout with oil, which greatly increases the filter's ability to trap and hold dirt and dust. Filter oils are designed to be extremely tacky, which helps them trap and hold the dirt and helps the oil stay put. Think about the air velocity at full throttle! You should consider the foam filter to be the framework which holds the filter oil in place. Keep your favorite in your lube box. Aha, I hear you thinking, "I should get a second air filter, keep it clean and oiled and stored in a plastic bag or container, for weekends, dusty days or when I just haven't had a chance to get to the dirty one and I want to go riding tomorrow but just lost two hours, two knuckles, several hearty chunks of flesh and part of a fingernail doing my first ever tire change." Yes, indeed.

## Stands

While some dirt bikes come with an attached kickstand (side stand), the majority don't. Those that don't, do come with a stand that connects to the bike at the rear axle or by the footpeg. But when you get to spinning wrenches on your pride and joy, you'll quickly find that you want the bike vertical, rather than leaning as when using a side stand and you want to be able to get either or both wheels off the ground, if not actually raise the bike off the ground far enough to be able to work without hunching over.

*As with every dirt bike accessory, the range of offerings is incredible, with something for every budget.*

Fear not, the array of bike stands is impressive and covers every desire. They can seem expensive, but are generally worth every penny. The cheap way out is to build your own, or acquire an abandoned milk crate. These used to have metal frames and plastic bottoms and when stood on end, with the opening towards the front wheel, do a barely adequate job. The most useful and expensive stands raise your bike all the way up to where you can work on it from a standing position.

You'll see riders with bikes without side stands use a tie down and their pickup to park a bike without leaning it against the truck. The tie down simply goes from the normal attachment points inside the bed, to the normal hook-in spot on the handlebars and the bike is leaned away from the truck, constrained by the tie down.

## A Way to Transport Your Bike

Unless your motorcycle is street legal and it is not too far to where you're going riding off-road, or you ride only on your own property, you'll need a way to carry it, something like a pick-up truck, a van, a trailer or a very good friend with one who always wants to ride with you wherever you go.

If you were to search the archives of the dirt bike publications, you could collect a fascinating array of unique transportation schemes. Long ago, when car bumpers were made of steel, you could buy bumper racks which bolted on. Each held one wheel. I used them on the back of a '65 Plymouth Valiant to haul my Ossa Stiletto. Plenty of folks, including yours truly, were perfectly willing to disassemble the bike into major subassemblies in order to cram it into a station wagon, the trunk, even the back seat. Dirt bike riders fully understand the motto, Adapt, Improvise, Overcome.

## Tie Downs

*Tie downs come in a wide variety of colors and quality. Bikes are expensive; tie downs are relatively cheap. Spring for good ones.*

To transport your bike, you'll need to hold it in place. Not to say that it is invalid to simply lay it on its side, maybe with a cushion underneath. It just lacks a certain cool factor. The standard way is with tie downs. These are heavy duty (you can tow a car with a couple of them) fabric straps with steel hooks on each end and a locking mechanism released by pressing a lever. The locking mechanism is attached to one hook by a short section of strap. A much longer length of strap with the other hook on the end passes through the locking mechanism. Wherever the strap is pulled through within the locking mechanism, it will stay there under tremendous load unless the release is pressed. Tie down designs intended for cargo (ratcheting types) certainly will work, but are clumsy to use for this purpose. Heck, rope works too.

Tie downs are connected between the handlebars and secure points in the transport vehicle. The bike should be roughly centered between the secure points and these need to be far enough apart so that the straps create wide triangles to the bike. Triangles equal stability. If the straps are too vertical, the bike can and will tip over during your drive. Think of the angle as the strap is pulling the bike out as well as down. Now go a step further. The straps also need to be angled forward, at least in line with the front axle, so that they also pull the bike forward. You'll quickly arrive at a standard layout for your vehicle, for one, up to the maximum number of bikes you've figured out how to cram in. When you're trying a new setup, remember, down, apart and forward.

Hook the short end of the strap over the handlebars, inside of the crossbar if the bars have one, but basically above the tops of the forks. The locking mechanisms will be just below the bars. Press the lever and pull the other hook so that the tie down is long enough to reach the secure attachment point. Some put a twist in the strap to minimize fluttering if the bike will be in the wind. When both straps are in place, pull the strap's loose ends so as to shorten and thus tighten them. Alternate pulling each strap. You can push on the associated side of the handlebar to help get them tighter. It is not necessary to bring the fender all the way down to the tire, just enough to get the bike to feel solid.

Tie the loose end you were pulling on into a neat half hitch right at/below the locking mechanism. This way, if the locking mechanism should slip (everything fails eventually), this will prevent the strap from loosening. It also bundles up the loose end so that it doesn't flap in the wind and spank the cool graphics on your radiator wings 93 trillion times on your way to the trails.

Some swear by putting a block (wood) or a partially inflated ball (soccer or volley) between the front tire and the fender and pull the bike down tight against it, so as to not put a constant load on the forks, this seems more valid the longer the trip. There are products available which were designed for this task. Others detest marring their bars with the hooks, or the locking mechanism might rub on the radiator wings and employ a simple loop of the same fabric strap to move the connection point of the tie down away from the bike. Note: on open rail trailer setups, you must also tie the rear wheel into the channel, or it will bounce out with unpleasant consequences. Some small trucks with short beds require three tie downs.

Bikes are relatively expensive, tie downs are cheap. Don't buy cheap tie downs, get good ones. When they start to fray and die, toss them.

## Bike Shoes

*A Bike Shoe. The locking arm has yet to be swung all the way over the tire towards the bike.*

These are another method of holding a bike in a vehicle. Steel or aluminum, they basically hold the front wheel down with a metal loop over the front tire. An over-center cam design, operated by a second metal loop, locks it in place. I have a set and they've never failed me. They do need to be bolted into the vehicle, which can prevent other uses. I have seen folks attach them to plywood, which the weight of the front wheel tends to hold down, but tie downs are then also (lightly) applied. While the notion is valid, if the front wheel is stuck in one place the rest of the bike ain't going anywhere, there is some bike movement visible at the handlebars while you drive. I always added tie downs, lightly loaded, to stop the motion. Besides, bikes are expensive, tie downs are . . . you know this saying now.

## Ramp

Ramps are available in steel or aluminum, black or natural. You can buy a purpose designed unit or get some aluminum channel from a metal distributor, or just use a 2X6. In the end, you'll be glad to get one designed for the job, the angled lip, traction provided by the holes and other touches minimize loading accidents.

*Ramps come in all colors, shapes and lengths.*

Some dudes are buff enough to simply pick the bike up and set it into the back of the pickup. Offroad champion Scott Summers was the poster boy bike hoister. Or you can carefully pop a nearly stationary wheelie and set the front wheel on the tailgate and then lift the rear wheel up. Not for beginners.

With a little less strength you can pick up the front wheel and set it on the tailgate, without dropping the bike and then hoist the rear wheel up. We're still talking young and buff and probably at the beginning of the day rather than after a hard ride.

## Tips On Loading Your Bike in Your Vehicle

*A bike on its way up the ramp into a pickup. Notice the crate placed so as to be a helping step up into the bed.*

All your plans for how you'll transport your bike(s) must focus on protecting the bikes and not damaging your vehicle (handlebar dents from the inside out on the side of a van are pretty obvious oopsies). Maximizing tie down triangulation and front-wheel stability are the key factors, along with realizing that the "system" will sway and give some.

An 8' pickup truck can hold four full-size bikes, barely. The bikes need to be offset, alternately, from the front of the truck bed, using milk crates, wood blocks, whatever, in order for the handlebars to offset. Old knobbies or other suitable materials placed generally around the engine areas prevent bike-to-bike rubbing, but any time you pack them in tight there will be some minor impact. Every bike still needs to be tied down and you'll have fun stringing the straps under fenders and through wheels. You do want the tie downs to run in as straight a line as possible from the bars to the anchor point. In essence, you want to end up with all four tied down as a big unit. The outer bikes outside tie downs will have almost no triangulation effect, thus the need to bundle them up. Four bikes can also be arranged with two pulled forward and two toward the tail gate, again alternating them, but this sometimes loads up the tailgate's latch mechanism with bad short- and/or long-term results. Besides, it just seems to add risk to rely on the tailgate.

*Here's a shot with two bikes loaded. Note the to-the-side and forward triangulation of the tie downs. Note that the outer tie downs have minimal to-the-side triangulation. Note the gap between the bars, so that if the bikes sway, they won't hit.*

While one bike would seemingly best be loaded in the center, and that is fine, on most trucks you'll find the forward wall of the bed bowing towards the cab soon enough. Off-setting the bike to the left towards the driver's side a bit helps prevent this and clears the view out the center mirror, without detracting much from tie down triangulation effectiveness. There are bed-stiffener products available.

Two bikes, in order to clear the handlebar ends, will actually be far enough outboard that the outer tie downs have minimal triangulation. Snug them down extra tight. If you think the bar ends might bounce off of each other, offset the bikes, or if they both have bark busters, tie them tightly together. That unitizes the bikes and is very effective inside a van.

In short bed pickups there are two schools of thought. Some put the bike in diagonally (thus one only will fit) and use three tie downs to triangulate it in place, allowing the tailgate to be closed. In my experience, it has always been fine to leave the tailgate down; the rear wheel rests at the junction of the gate and the bed and is supported well. Of course, everything else placed in the bed must be secured by blockage, bungee or something. There are many products available which essentially form a fence around an open tailgate.

A long full-size van can hold three bikes (at least). Even some mini-vans can hold a bike or two. A tie down between the bars and front axle can hold the forks compressed to help get them through smaller doors (this works on very tall pick-up canopy/shells, too).

## The Basic 3-Rail Trailer

There are a jillion trailer configurations. Most basic is the "rail" version – an axle, a basic frame tying it to the hitch which provides a platform for one to four and typically three metal channels (rails). The u-shaped channels are just wider than motorcycle tires and are bent up or otherwise provide a stop for the front tire. There should be points to attach the tie downs which will pull the bikes forward and out. In three- and four-rail models, the rails are offset fore and aft to clear handlebars. Do not neglect to firmly attach the rear wheel within its rail! A piece of rope, a very heavy-duty, solid rubber strap type of bungee, make it secure. They will bounce out if you don't do this.

Flat-floored trailers, especially if they have low or half-height walls, are extremely flexible (they can be used for a lot more than bike hauling, too). On some, the front wall is a suitable front tire stop, although you can tie down a bike without a stop. A straight pull back with a tie down from a foot peg mount or a lower frame rail acts as the "stop." The normal front tie downs attached from the handlebars pull the bike forward against the rear one. This can also be done by pulling both fore and aft from the handlebars, again trapping the bike, but it takes four tie downs, two per side, to do this successfully.

Box trailers are like a van, you mainly have to consider handlebar-to-wall and bike-to-bike impacts during swaying.

## Fanny Pack

If you ride more than a mile from your transport, or let's just say, farther than you'd prefer to push a recalcitrant machine, then you need to carry some tools and spare parts with you. This can be as basic as a spare plug and a wrench. At the other extreme, expert offroaders create custom pack contents with all of their favorite spares. The industry has also responded with a wide array of custom space-saving dirt bike tools.

## Handguards

Personally, I'd run these on every bike. I feel a little exposed without them. Handguards are simple aluminum bar protectors that mount from the ends of the handlebars to an inboard section of the bars, enclosing your hands and the controls at the ends of the bars. Absolutely worthless are plastic designs which simply mount to the clutch and brake lever pivot points, except for their moderate wind/rain/roost protection. Hit anything and they'll pivot in, smashing fingers, disengaging the clutch and/or locking the front brake.

*The basic metal (aluminum) handguard is a band attached at the end of the bars and inboard along the bars.*

The good ones are simply an aluminum bar running between the mounting points, some also have some added width via over-molded plastic sections. They can be lightly bent to accommodate variations in handlebar shape. Most important, be sure to select ones intended for your bar type, steel vs. aluminum, regular vs. oversize. The cam-type mounting devices for the inside of the ends of the bars and the clamps for the inboard part of the bars, must be the correct size to function.

Handguards do a lot more than protect your pinkies from getting smacked when you wend too close to a tree. They can save your hands and wrists in slide out and lay down crashes, if you train yourself to keep your hands on the bars in those instances, which is also good because you maintain control of the clutch and throttle and can keep the bike running regardless. In my experience, they also seem to strengthen handlebars through triangulation.

In all fairness, some opine that they can ensnare your hands and injure your wrists in over-the-bars crashes. In my opinion, you should let go and be looking for a place to roll or slide upon landing from your short flight.

For extremely wet or muddy conditions, you can install large oversized protectors, affectionately called "elephant ears." While they may look funny, they work, keeping your hands dry and clean, keeping you in control in nasty conditions. They work best in concert with handguards, which keep these big sails from being pressed back against your hands at speed.

## Dirt Bike Stickers

Stickers are a core part of this sport. I imagine a team of psychiatrists could expound at length on why; let's just skip it. Every bike manufacturer, every aftermarket part and gear manufacturer, every distributor, every shop, organization and club, every event, even a bunch of sticker manufacturers, all make stickers touting their shtick. And we put them in four key places;

our transport vehicle's rear window, on the bikes, on the toolbox and all over the fridge in the shop.

*A tiny array of the universe of dirt bike stickers, tastefully arranged around the sticker from a famous NW off-road racing club.*

Make no mistake, this is serious art. On the bike and transport vehicle, size, placement and arrangement are critical. The toolbox and the fridge? Well, intense coverage seems to be the goal.

On the bike and vehicle, there are two basic schools, those who only run the stickers for their sponsors and those who run whatever. Whatever seems to break down into those who apply every sticker from every product they buy or can otherwise score and those who narrow their selection so as to make some personal statement, usually alluding to how attractive or cool they feel they are. Posers.

## Dirt Bike T-Shirts

Just like stickers, every business and organization and event features T-shirts. These are as much a part of the core of the culture as stickers. You will find your collection grows rapidly. It will include "everyday" shirts and prized classics. I will admit to still having as many as I have ever worn out or lost and there are over 200 stacked in the closet. You do the math.

## Dirt Bike Hats

The marketing goes on. My collection is more limited, compared to my shirts, but still numbers several dozen.

*A small sampling of the trillions of dirt bike hats that have been created.*

## Dirt Bike Publications

Like every activity from stamp collecting to deep sea diving, an active specialized press plays with the balance between informing

*A few publications from the vast available library.*

the reader/participant and supporting the industry. You will be a rare rider in deed if you don't become a subscriber to at least one.

## Dirt Bike Videos

These products began with the monumental "On Any Sunday," shot by surfing cinematographer Bruce Brown. They didn't really go far for many years, mostly racing series recaps, but because Brown did such a fantastic job of capturing the essence of off-road dirt bike riding, there was little left for future filmmakers to explore. Then came the jump videos. Pundits debate whether extreme jumping and in-the-air gymnastic tricks, including not even touching the bike, led to this boom in the dirt bike video industry, or if the cameras spawned the extreme riding.

## Dirt Bike Games

Oh yeah, these days you can get some pretty fine dirt bike video games for your computer or your game playing box connected to your TV. Better the kids fantasize riding a bike than blowing people away, eh? The technology has passed the threshold wherein experienced riders find these games to be both realistic (except for perhaps the stunt portions) and fun. The later the release, generally the better the game, although there are still some real duds out there. Ask at your shop, they'll know which ones are hot.

# CHAPTER 5

## *LEARNING TO RIDE*

It's time to get to the point and learn to ride! From this point on, the student rider should wear all their gear through every lesson. Start that critical habit NOW.

Here is where we'll diverge from the way folks typically teach their friends to ride. Usually, the brakes are pointed out and the basic concept of the shifter are explained and then it is immediately on to attempting to ride under power. This simply leads to disaster too often and doesn't build good habits from the beginning.

Brake training first - I'm gonna beg you to follow this advice, to learn to operate the brakes and practice with them and master them, before you ever start the engine.

Second, clutch it - another key step before roaring off on your bike is to master and understand the feel of the clutch. Just a few minutes at this will leapfrog you over likely dozens of embarrassing and difficult situations.

### Stability

There's a reason a barstool has at least three legs. A structure needs to rest on at least three points to be stable at rest. Physicists and mathematicians would simply say that three points determine a plane. Your bike sits on two points, one at each tire, and true to physics it will to fall over if not supported by the kickstand, your leg, or the insane balancing capabilities of a top trials rider. That is stability at rest. In motion, stability is greatly affected by the following two principles.

### Gyro

Spinning things create what physicists and mathematicians call a gyroscopic effect. That effect makes the spinning thing resist being tilted out of whatever plane it lies on. The faster it spins, the stronger this effect is. This useful phenomenon makes your bike want to stay more upright the faster it's going. It also makes it resist changing direction. So as you gain speed, your bike becomes more stable. This effect happens because of inertia.

## Inertia

Bodies at rest tend to stay at rest, bodies in motion tend to stay in motion. It takes application of a force to change the inertia of an object. For example, it takes force from the engine to get your bike moving, unless you supply the force by pushing, or use gravity by rolling downhill. Once moving, your bike would roll forever if friction and wind resistance weren't applying small forces to stop you.

The message behind this physics lesson is simple. You can overcome the natural instability of your bike at rest by riding it!

When stopped or going very slowly, your bike wants to fall down and it would rather cushion its fall by landing on your body. Simple exercise of your ability to balance isn't worthless, but it isn't going to keep you off the ground forever, either. When your bike is moving it gains stability, and the faster it moves the more stable it is.

Finally, consider turning. If you want to turn sharply, you have to slow down. Your bike will not allow you to rapidly change direction at high speed. Instead it will spit you off, unless you absorb and re-direct the excess energy by aligning it with the face of a banked surface.

## The Guide

You can teach yourself to control and ride a dirt bike by following the methods in this book, but it will be a lot easier if you have a knowledgeable rider around to guide you. I know I'm dreaming to think that someone who will help you learn to ride will also read this book, or even willingly follow the steps that you want to after reading it, but I do know that you will get off to a safer, stronger start if you and your guide do. Someone who really wants to help you learn will probably be willing to go along with these proven steps.

If you can't get started with a guide, a knowledgeable rider to chaperone you through your first dates with two wheeled freedom, you'll still be better off with a partner. In a pipe dream I see two guys, no wait, a young couple, getting their hands on a copy of this book, then two bikes, then setting off on to a lifetime of fun and adventure.

## Getting Started

A test of readiness to ride a dirt bike is a proven capability on a bicycle. It doesn't matter how old you are, if you can't ride a bicycle you shouldn't be trying to ride a motorcycle. The basic feeling of balance on two wheels, that it is steadier as you pick up speed, is something you should be at ease with before adding a motor to the mix. Slow speed steering-to-turn and higher speed countersteer-to-turn are just as critical and best learned at bicycle velocities. Even better if your skill is such that there's been a playful lock-up-the-rear and skid and some little wheelies over bumps built into your pedal pushing repertoire.

## Steering Basics

This is another subject you need to be exposed to before you move on to learning to ride, and it will be reinforced as needed in the lessons that follow.

But for a few very skilled bicycle riders, the notion of countersteering pedal pushers doesn't exist. When you think of turning your bicycle, you think of turning the bars to the left to go left and right to go right. This is only true for very low speeds (under ten mph) and it is the same for a motorcycle. At higher speeds on your bicycle, you think of leaning left to turn left and leaning right to turn right.

This is NOT how to turn a motorcycle at speeds greater than ten mph or so. You must countersteer, or you are not truly in control of your bike as you turn. This is true on street bikes as well.

Countersteering means that the bars are turned, at least slightly, to the right to turn left and to the left to turn right. What!?! I am not going to explain the physics. You must trust all experienced riders from all time and stay with me on this.

We'll take a left turn to explain how to countersteer. A left turn at anything but the very slowest speeds is initiated by pushing on the left handlebar. This begins to force the left side of the bike down, as well as slightly turning the wheel to the right. But the lean carries much more turning effect than the wheel angle. Stay with the bike as it leans over, don't "lead" the leaning action with your body. You will also note that as you are turning left, the bars are turned slightly to the right. Don't "freeze" the bars in any position as you go through the turn. Stay loose and in control. Pressing harder on the left side of the bars will both push the bike further down and increase countersteer and you will turn tighter. Lessening pressure will do the opposite. Response is instant.

Turning without countersteering, just by leaning and holding the bars stuck in one position, will result in being stuck on the initial line and if a bump in the turn lessens traction or the throttle is rolled on too soon, the bike will slide out or spin around.

## Lesson 1 – First Moves

### Getting On and Off the Bike

Don't neglect this little lesson, it will come in handy immediately. Remember that what seems obvious to one is something all new to another. Take the time to help good habits get started.

While standing on either side of the bike, but typically from the left side, hold the bike in a set position by applying the front brake. In one smooth motion, swing the right leg over the seat and sit on the bike, both feet on the ground, still applying the front brake. Lean the bike slightly to the left, so that it is balanced between the left leg and the wheels. Pick up the right foot and place it on the foot peg. Actuate the rear brake, release the front brake. Switch feet. Always have one or both brakes applied unless you intend for the bike to be able to roll.

When getting off the bike, start by applying the front brake. In general people seem to naturally dismount to the left, though it doesn't really matter. If you go for the left, lean the bike to that side with your left foot down and balance in that position. Stay smooth and swing your right leg over and off the seat to the ground.

Note how you use the front brake to control the possible movement of the bike as you get on, off, or stand with either foot. Make it a habit.

## Basic Sitting Position

Now that you can get on and off the bike without total embarrassment, let's go over the basic seated riding position. Later I will describe the proper (standing) riding position, but for your initial riding lesson we'll stick with sitting.

*The basic sitting riding position, viewed from the side; forward on the seat, elbows out.*

Put your bike on a stand, lean it against a wall with a handlebar end, lean it off your truck with a tie down, or have a helper hold it. Get on and sit down on the seat. Put your feet on the pegs and rest the balls of your feet (the wide portion between your toes and your arches) on the pegs. Slide all the way forward to the front of the seat, at the seat-tank junction. Rest your hands on the grips, as far inboard (toward the center) as the grips allow. Extend your middle and forefingers and rest them on top of the brake and clutch levers. Raise your elbows up, out and away from your body a bit. Lean forward slightly. There you have it, the basic sitting position.

*The sitting position, viewed from the front. Get those elbows up and out.*

In this position, squeeze the clutch and brake levers. The brake lever should stop or get very difficult to move at or before the point where it contacts your ring and pinkie fingers. The clutch lever will go all the way to the bars if those fingers were not in the way. This should be plenty of lever motion to allow full clutch function. While resting your fingers on the levers, operate the throttle. Note that without "over-grabbing" the throttle, your elbow drops low and contorts you into a less than comfortable position when you open the throttle all the way. From early on you will only be using a small part of the throttle's total movement, so don't worry about over-grabbing for now. Over-grabbing is where you reach "past" the throttle, so that when your hands reach the neutral basic position, the throttle is already opened some.

Operate the rear brake, and note that you have to move your foot forward on the peg to reach the tip of the lever. Slip your left toe below and above the tip of the shift lever to use it.

We'll use this basic sitting position until you get past the basic riding lessons, after which you should use the advanced riding position described later at all times if possible.

*Overgrabbing the throttle as it is first grasped, so that at a mid-to-full throttle open position, the right elbow will be in the correct position.*

## Lesson 2 – The Brakes and Shifter

The first thing a person learns about a new activity seems to be something they naturally return to in a crisis. Anyone who has ever taught more than a few folks to ride has seen a rider panic and twist the throttle wide open as they careen into the weeds or worse. It is much better if a new rider instinctively operates the brakes when they panic.

I cannot tell you how much you will appreciate this. Learn the brakes thoroughly and first.

Consider also that the following lesson allows the guide to quickly judge whether the rider and bike are appropriately matched, i.e., can control be demonstrated in the easiest conditions the rider will encounter?

### Find a Hill

It really helps to have a gentle hill, one that slopes so that a bike will get rolling and gently accelerate down. If not, you need to push the bike/rider through this step. Hint: grab a helper if you do. With one of you on each side of the rear of the bike, each with one hand on the seat and one on the rear fender, you'll help balance as well as push.

It doesn't take a long hill, just one long enough to get the bike rolling along. Needless to say (I hope), towing is not an option here.

Obviously, you have to get the bike to the top of the hill if you're using one. If it is a long hill, drive it up in the truck. If it is a short one push it up together, or the guide can ride it up.

Position the bike so that it's pointing down the hill (or in the direction you intend to push). Get on the bike. You should be able to without help (use the front brake!). Balance the bike with your left foot down. "Cover" (move your foot forward into position) the rear brake lever. Practice squeezing the front brake lever and pushing the rear brake pedal simultaneously, always pulling in the clutch lever every time you operate the brakes.

Take a deep breath, for this is your first ride! Remember, the engine must be OFF!

Release both brakes slowly, letting the bike start to roll. Walk the bike between your legs to help it get going if you need to. Just as it starts to roll, pull in the clutch, apply both brakes, and stop the bike. We're going to get you into the habit of always pulling that clutch in so that you don't continuously stall the engine when you progress to the powered stage.

Ease the bike down the hill, repeating the above process. Go a little faster and farther. Concentrate on feeling the brakes- they aren't just on-off switches. Realize that you can stop the bike with very gentle pressure. Find the point where each brake just starts to release. Don't increase your rolling speed or distance any more than is needed to get moving under your own balance.

A good test of how well you can feel the brakes is to increase the distance you roll before stopping, without increasing your speed. Do this with brake control by releasing them enough to roll, but "feathering" them (increasing gentle pressure up to and around the point where they start to engage) to maintain a constant speed. If you feel yourself slowing, release pressure slightly, if speeding up, apply more. Are you pulling in the clutch every time you use the brakes?

Next try holding the bike in position on the hill with the rear brake only. Then roll farther down the hill, using the rear brake only. Keep the speed and distance as before, then try rolling farther but not faster again. Do not try it with only the front brake yet.

What! Why? Front brake stopping exposes a phenomenon driven by physics, there is no avoiding it. When the steering (front) wheel of a bike (or a four wheeled vehicle, for that matter) stops rolling and starts sliding, the bike will tend to continue in the direction it was headed when traction was lost, regardless of which way the wheel is subsequently turned. The transition between rolling and steering and skidding and not steering can be very subtle and sudden depending on speed and available traction. The same is true for the rear wheel, too.

Okay. Now try it with the front brake, gently and only with the bike vertical. If it is leaned over, the front tire is more likely to break traction (start to slide or skid). In the event of a front tire skid, immediately release the front brake. Be prepared to use the rear brake if you don't like what is happening.

For your final braking lesson, understand that 80% of your stopping power comes from the front brake. When a bike is braking, all the weight shifts forward, pressing the front tire into the ground. The rear of the bike tends to un-weight and the rear brake will easily lock up the rear wheel. As soon as it breaks traction and starts to skid, it is no longer doing much stopping. Under very hard braking, while in the standing riding position, shifting your weight to the rear helps to overcome this.

When you start actually riding the motorcycle under power, continue to develop the habit of always using both brakes (and always pulling in the clutch).

Keep at the braking practice until you have them all down. This may happen in a few cycles, or it may require lots of reps. Don't rush it. Master them. As you gain confidence, start increasing your speed and distance.

When you have mastered the brakes, you should be able to get the bike rolling fast enough and/or hit the rear brake hard enough to skid the rear wheel to a stop (the particularly astute will notice that this can lengthen stopping distance). Do not skid the front wheel!

### Shifter Operation

The shifter is operated with your left foot, specifically the big toe. The mantra is simple; lift up – shift up (next higher gear), push down – shift down (next lower gear). The machine will only shift one gear in either direction, from the gear you are currently in, per shifter move. This is not like a car, where you could shift directly from fourth, to say, first, in one move.

Further, neutral can only be found between $1^{st}$ (a partial upshift) and $2^{nd}$ (a partial downshift). You cannot shift from first to high or high to first. The pattern is not a full circle.

Dirt bikes can be shifted without operating the clutch, especially on an upshift, which some bikes can even do while under full throttle.

It is as simple as that. The footpeg acts as a fulcrum for the rotation of your toe, upshift or downshift.

While the mechanism is quite rugged and the designers fully understand that you are wearing a very heavy boot and will be making shifts under violent conditions, you should still develop a habit from the start of not pounding or stomping on the shifter, but instead making deliberate, smooth shifting actions.

It is especially hard on your tranny when at a stop and in neutral to rev the engine and then stomp it into first. Let the motor return to idle or near it before you make this shift, especially when the bike has just been warmed up! If you are trying to overcome an operational difficulty (bike stalls due to a clutch issue, for example), then it's okay to keep the revs up a bit as you shift into gear. You can indeed get a bike going with some pushing then shifting into first, without the clutch functioning at all if need be.

## Lesson 3 – Starting the Engine

Your bike's engine can be started in several ways. The basic plan is to use the kickstarter, but you might have electric start or both. Or neither. The fallback plan, although you will find yourself using it on purpose, is the bump start.

The main goal of any engine starting method is to get the engine spinning, i.e. the piston moving up and down. If all else falls in place the piston will suck in an air-fuel charge, compress it as a spark appears across the plug gap, and the resulting explosion will drive the piston down, pushing the crankshaft around to do it again all by itself.

There are some tricks to be learned, lest you develop and exercise the vocabulary of the fabled dock hand.

### Starting a Cold Engine

Engines run on a mixture of air and gasoline where the gas droplets are minute, almost like a fog. Cold metal and air tend to force gas droplets to condense out of the air they are suspended in, so cold engines need a little extra gas.

Every bike made comes with some form of choke mechanism. While this is a good name for the device on the carburetor on your car, it is a complete misnomer for the one on your bike. Let's skip the detailed explanation of the car side. On a bike's carb, the choke is a device that opens up a passageway around the main throat as well as an easy fuel supply to that passageway. A piston sucking past this passageway, with the throttle closed and blocking the carb's main throat, will draw in an air-fuel mixture heavy on the fuel.

So a choke is a system designed to use a cycling piston's normal sucking in of air-fuel mixture to richen or even slightly flood that mixture with gas. Many a European bike in the 60s and 70s had a carb with a tickler button. Pushing it would simply allow fuel to flow right into the intake. You'd soon learn how many counts to hold it in for different starting situations.

While some brand new models are switching to Fuel Injection, where the choke function is handled automatically, your bike is likely to be "normally aspirated," or have a carb, and thus a manual choke. It is operated with a lever or a push-pull knob, which is located either on the carburetor or near the center of the handlebars. If it is a knob in either location, the choke is applied by pulling up/out on it and turned off by pushing it back down/in. Levers can be trickier— sometimes you lift up, sometimes you push down, and the least intuitive require you to lift up and over a cam lock. While some levers have an indicator printed on or near them, others will require referring to your manual, or if all else fails, trial and error.

### Let's Get Her Started!

First, knowing that you have plenty of fuel in the tank and otherwise have inspected your bike and believe it is in good running condition, turn the petcock to ON. Find and operate your choke and make sure your kill switch is not activated.

Don't, I repeat, do not touch the throttle whenever the choke is engaged! When you start kicking or otherwise turning the engine over, if you can't resist slightly opening the throttle, move your right hand to the left, on the bars, away from it altogether. On some modern four strokes this is even more critical than on two strokes.

Position the kickstarter, place your foot on it and gently move it downward until resistance is felt, then release it and let it come back up. This positions everything in the engine and mechanism for maximum kickstarter effectiveness. Now you will kick it all the way through until it stops moving, usually by hitting the right footpeg. This is not a slap motion, indeed, the word "kick" doesn't accurately describe what you want to do. Raise your body up and forward and use a combination of your whole body moving downward and extending your leg from a bent position to straightened. Use smooth, powerful, individual kicks. Rapidly repeated slaps will result in mistiming or movement and wasted kickstarter gears and/or shins. Pretty much gone are the days of bikes which often backfired and kickstart mechanisms that would translate that energy into a reverse motion of the kickstarter. Believe it, I have seen and experienced being catapulted up and over the bars (often leading to leg and knee injuries).

*The kickstarter is swung out, away from the bike, moved gently down until resistance is felt, released (ratcheted) back to the top of its stroke to maximize leverage and is ready to kick.*

Repeat. Repeat. Continue repeating. This should, with dang near every bike known, result in the bike starting or certainly sounding like it is trying to start, after no more than three to ten solid attempts. If it doesn't, then something else is wrong and you are going to have to figure it out before going any farther.

Assuming that it started, you should do nothing. The bike should idle all by itself for a while at a higher than normal rpm. Usually you should let it run, untouched, for ten to fifteen seconds. Sometimes you'll have to restart it once or twice until it runs by itself and, on a bike way out of tune, you may have to fiddle with everything and nurse it to life. Here's hoping that you aren't embarking on your dirt bike career with a machine in such poor condition. Regardless, you'll get it with practice. Remember to believe that they WANT to run.

The transition from "cold" to "warm" can be easy or it can be touchy, depending on the bike, the temperature and a thousand other factors. If all goes well, you'll simply turn the choke off and the bike will revert to its standard idle. You'll blip the throttle now and then, gingerly at first and then purposefully, testing its warmth by its ability to rev freely, maybe even briefly holding it wide open to help clean it out.

There are many variations to the cold-warm transition. Some chokes have an intermediate position that can be useful. Going back and forth between choke on and choke off, or simply holding the idle at a higher level with the throttle for a moment or two are also familiar techniques.

Warm it up! Don't just start the bike and take off riding as soon as you can get it off the choke. You will quite likely stick the piston in the cylinder or at the least accelerate wear. A water-cooled bike should be warmed up for three full minutes, an air-cooled one for at least one. The cylinder and pipe should be warm to the touch, if not getting too hot to touch (hint: don't touch it, just put your hand near the surface). Many older air-cooled four strokes are notoriously slow to warm up and will refuse to run right until after a few minutes as well.

### Starting a Warm Engine

If your bike is still warm because you rode it and parked it for a while at a trail junction waiting for the laggards, waiting for the gun in a dead engine start or just to take a breather, it should start in one or two kicks. Throttle position under these conditions will vary by bike, most like either a fully-closed or slightly-cracked open throttle. Everyone seems to learn their bike very quickly. The choke is not needed.

When you're starting a warm bike because you've just picked it up off the ground, the experience can range from no sweat to buckets full. Maybe you'll be lucky and she'll respond like she is simply warm, but it won't always be that way.

What should you try when it won't light off? If it's a two stroke, try full throttle. Open her wide and kick it through a few times. If she fires, ease off the throttle immediately and all will return to normal. If it is a modern, water-cooled racing four stroke you may have to use a "hot start button" to prime the engine. These are either a red knob on the side of the carb, or a small lever on the left side of the bars, above the clutch. These allow extra air into the engine.

*Modern four stroke engines often have a hot start system, to help you start a stalled, but warm, engine. The red knob with "pull" on it is the hot start knob on this Yamaha.*

Most of all, when you are struggling, keep changing tactics every three or four kicks. Besides throttle position (full on or completely off), there are two other tricks, using the choke and closing the petcock. Turning on the choke will add extra fuel to the equation, to help overcome an empty float bowl drained while upside down. Never try this for more than a few kicks. Shutting off the petcock attempts to overcome a flooded bottom end, where the contents of the float bowl have taken advantage of your failure to adhere to "shiny side up, rubber side down" to slither past the reeds into the crankcase. Open the throttle wide and this may take quite a few kicks to take effect. Then try it at other throttle positions, then re-open the petcock. If you think she is completely flooded, remove the spark plug, turn off the petcock and press the kill switch while holding the throttle wide open and kicking her over. I have seen massive sprays of gas blow out of the plug hole in cases like this.

*The small lever above the clutch lever is the hot start system on this KTM.*

Keep trying new stuff. Never rush it. Don't fail to properly position the kickstarter and to kick firmly and all the way through. If you get tired and can't kick properly, rest. Never get frustrated. In general, only one thing besides some form of crash damage can keep you stopped cold and that's a fouled or drenched plug.

### Electric Start Machines

Ah, the magic button. Offering electric start has been common with four stroke machines, especially the off-road vs. MX versions, as there is a weight penalty with the starter and battery. It seems now like every brand offers at least an electric start version of each engine displacement, while some make this feature standard.

It's simple, just push it. Cold— choke on, don't you dare touch the throttle. Warm— some bikes respond best to the throttle being open a bit, some still demand it be closed. Don't forget the hot start button after a crash.

Just like with the family car but faster, holding the start button down continuously without the bike starting will quickly drain the battery. Attempt to start the bike with short, 3-5 second attempts and wait 5-10 seconds between attempts. You will be very chagrined to run your battery down if your model is one that doesn't include a kickstarter and may be almost as bummed even if it does, for the effectiveness of the boot operated method may be low.

## Starting in Gear

Yes, Matilda, this is possible in any gear. Simply pull the clutch all the way to the bars and start it. But it won't be as easy as with the bike in neutral, because there will be some residual drag through the clutch. It generally works with a recently stopped, not-crashed bike.

## The Bump Start

These are methods of starting the bike that are based on forcing the engine to cycle by getting the rear wheel rotating while the bike is in gear. The bump start is simple and useful, and skilled riders will often take advantage of it as a quick way to get her lit while also starting to roll, or to restart an engine they stalled while in motion. Otherwise, these methods are generally employed to get a damaged bike running and back to the truck, or to try to get a stubborn bike running at all. A very long hill bump start is also capable of cleaning out a flooded bike without having to change the spark plug . . . sometimes. This is not appropriate for a beginning rider and is only included here for your future reference.

This takes a hill, the longer the better. With your bike at the top of the hill, point her downhill and ensure that everything is ready for the motor to run (gas in the tank, petcock on and so forth). Get her rolling downhill in neutral. Stand on the pegs, pull in the clutch, open the throttle a bit and get ready. The next steps need to be done in rapid (depending on the length and steepness of the hill) sequence. Shift UP, to second, at least, third if you can. Simultaneously release the clutch and bounce your butt down on the seat, hard. Being in a gear higher than first will help prevent the rear wheel from locking up and skidding and coming down on the seat with all your weight as the clutch is released helps push the tire hard against the ground. Once the engine is rotating, driven by the rear wheel, it will tend to keep doing so until the hill runs out. If you have time and it hasn't started, try different throttle positions (open her up, of course keeping your right fingers ready on the clutch).

A few more tips. Some bikes disengage so completely at the clutch that you can shift up to third before starting to roll down the hill. Some clutch designs drag such that you have to start the process in neutral and as soon as you upshift to second, the wheel will start trying to turn the motor, even before releasing the clutch.

If your kickstarter falls off or otherwise fails during a ride, ditto your electric start, always do your rest stops at the top of some hill or grade.

When you get good at this, it will amaze you how short a hill will do the trick, as the motor will fire off in a revolution or two.

### Push Starting

While I have seen this done solo, generally as a running bump start on too shallow a hill, it usually takes at least one helper. The duo gets the bike ready to run and while in neutral, pushes to get it rolling as fast as possible and then the rider does the bump start routine. If the rider was also a pusher (at first), it will be up to the remaining pusher(s) to continue to simulate a hill while the rider goes through the bump start portion of this method. Here getting quickly to third really helps, since the pushers are not going to last long against lower gear engine compression.

There are a lot of minor variations of push starting. The rider starting as a pusher may do a side-saddle routine, to hasten getting to the bump start portion of the process before his pusher's tongue hits the ground. Multiple pushers really help. Many a crew has been soundly entertained by the tongue dragging antics of three riders struggling to get a stubborn machine running on a hot day, especially if they don't know better than to not try this in first gear.

### Remember This About Starting

If you have sufficient compression (120psi or greater should do the trick— I have seen motors run with less then 100, but not very well) and the carburetor delivers a reasonable air-fuel mixture upon being presented with vacuum from the cylinder and a sufficiently strong spark happens at the right time, every time, an engine is capable of starting and running. More than one old mechanic has advised when trying to fix a non-starting motor, to make sure those things are right, rather than trying to figure out what is wrong.

Be patient. Experiment with throttle, choke and petcock positions. Change every few kicks: full throttle/no choke, choke/no throttle, half throttle.  Pull the plug, close the petcock, open the throttle wide open, press the kill switch and kick the bad air through and out of the engine. Or let her cool completely down and start all over cold with the choke.

## Lesson 4 - The Clutch

Whereas most riders are simply shown the brakes, at which point their first riding lesson moves directly to getting the bike going in first gear, I encourage you to focus on one more lesson first. The clutch is a critical part of truly controlling a dirt bike. Riders who master the drills in this section avoid more, if not all, of the embarrassing period where most beginners take forever to get the bike moving, er, lurching and do so mostly by luck, stalling it more often than not. At your first tight turn, you'll use the clutch to gently feel your way around, rather than the near impossible lurching you'll get from the throttle. Believe it, a feel for how the subtle use of the clutch is the most effective way to be in total control of the bike at every instant is best implanted in your brain from the beginning.

When riding your bike over any type of terrain, be it track or trail, you will find yourself wanting to quickly change how much power you are applying to the rear wheel. Turning the throttle will accomplish this, but not instantly in most situations. It takes time (multiple revolutions) for a new carburetor slide position to allow the piston to draw in a bigger fuel-air charge, and then for the engine to respond with acceleration/de-acceleration. Instead, if the engine is running at an rpm which will produce plenty of power relative to the needs of the immediate section of terrain, the amount of power transferred to the rear wheel can be instantly changed with subtle changes in clutch engagement.

Onward to the clutch! If the new rider is astride an automatic transmission-equipped bike, don't skip this lesson! Go to the end of the Walking the Bike Around section and apply that drill, then come back to the complete clutch exercise when the rider moves to a manual tranny.

## Never Let It All The Way Out

The object of this clutch lesson is to move and control the motion of the bike without ever letting the clutch lever out all the way, and thus realize the feeling of varied levels of clutch engagement and learn to truly finesse it. It is not an on/off switch. It can and must be engaged and disengaged to whatever extent is correct and appropriate for the immediate riding situation. In this exercise, once the bike is running and is in gear, the clutch will either be pulled all the way in or released out to the point where the bike will just begin to move forward.

If the new rider cannot accomplish limiting the range the clutch is moved to, use a plastic tie, twine, or something similar to limit the amount it can be released to just beyond the point of engagement.

On many bikes this lesson also requires holding the throttle open slightly, somewhere above idle, lest this drill become a frustrating cycle of stalls and restarts.

If the new rider cannot hold the throttle slightly open, one alternative is to turn the idle up instead. Another is to help the new rider stand on the right side of the motorcycle and hold the throttle open some. Don't worry, we'll be at walking speed for a while.

The guide needs to decide whether the student can control the clutch lever per the instructions given, not letting it all the way out while holding the throttle open some, or if a special bike setup is needed. The perfect setup will allow the clutch to reach the engagement point and slightly beyond without stalling the engine.

The bike should move forward at about a walking pace at maximum release with the clutch slipping some. You'll have to turn the idle up pretty high.

Don't get too hung up on this. Some bikes are easy to set up for a beginner, some aren't. Read the following lessons and you'll see the intent and you'll find a way to work through it. Always start with a review of the controls to be mastered and always place your hands correctly on the controls.

## Walking the Bike Around

The goal of this step is to come to the realization that absolute control of the clutch provides absolute control of the forward motion of the bike, that it is not an on-off switch, and that it instead rewards touch and finesse.

Start the bike in neutral. Apply the front brake, get off and stand on the left side. Hold the grips as though you were on the bike. Pull the clutch lever to the bars, step up to the left footpeg with your left foot and shift the bike down into first. Release the front brake and then ease the clutch lever out, just to the point where the clutch starts to engage, and immediately pull it back in to the bars.

*This rider is in the proper position to walk the bike around, using little throttle, never letting the clutch out all the way, completely controlling the forward motion of the bike with the clutch.*

Starts to engage! Where is that? Two things will let you know. You will feel the bike start to pull forward and you will hear the engine slow down slightly as the load is engaged.

Repeat a few times, always pulling it right back in, getting a feel for the point of engagement.

Now, slightly increase how far you let the clutch out so that the bike starts to roll forward, take a step along with it and pull the clutch right back in.

At your pace, work your way up to being able to get the bike to move along under its own power, at a very slow walk, by carefully controlling the clutch at or around the point of engagement. If anything isn't right, such as the bike gaining too much speed, getting out of control in any way, or the engine starting to stall, immediately pull the clutch to the bars.

Continue to work at this, walking your bike around under its own power. To make a loop in a confined area or just turn, always turn to the left (turn to the right in this position and a beginner will probably drop the bike).

As soon as possible, eliminate artificially limiting clutch travel. Be patient, as the student will suffer brain farts. If applicable, stop working the throttle for the beginner and/or return the idle to the standard position.

When the student is clearly in command of the throttle and clutch at no more than a walking speed, add in one more factor, if possible. Have the rider walk the bike under its own power up a shallow hill and turn to come down, but stop halfway through the turn using the front brake and, of course, pulling in the clutch. Prepare the rider to get the bike rolling and as the bike is pointing downhill, pull the clutch in, turn off the throttle and use the front brake to control the descent.

Repeat as needed, but do not fail to pay attention to the bike. It is getting worked and is not getting much cooling air over the cylinder or through the radiators. Work a few minutes at a time, then let the bike rest before repeating.

You should do the same basic walking practice with a new rider and an automatic transmission bike. The basics are the same, but the rider has to learn to walk the bike around by barely opening the throttle. The goal is control and they should soon learn to "feel" the automatic clutch engaging. If it appears that the student is tending to open the throttle too much, don't adjust the throttle cable to add a bunch of play and limit slide movement, or the rider will learn to twist it too wide open too soon. Instead, walk along and limit throttle movement with your hand.

### Finding Neutral

While the new rider is still basking in the glow of getting a real clue about the clutch and starts giving you the look, as in, "I want to ride it, NOW," make them learn to find neutral first.

Sit on the bike with the engine off, pull in the clutch and shift down to first. Note the change in lever movement in attempted downshifts after getting to first. It doesn't move as far and feels like it is hitting a hard stop. Let the clutch out and verify that the bike is in gear by trying to rock it forward and back, feeling the transmission and engine resist you.

Pull in the clutch and shift up to second. Rock it to verify. If it is not in gear, you accidentally found neutral! Yes, it is "hidden" halfway between first and second and it is found with a gentle, even weak, partial movement of the shift lever. Neutral can be reached from either first or second. If you didn't accidentally find neutral on that first upshift, now work at finding it. If you keep shifting too far, try gently rocking the bike forward and back, just a tiny bit, as you make the shift. This "unloads" the tranny and sometimes makes it easier to shift (especially if the motor is running). If you are still having trouble, get off and, with your helper holding the clutch in, work the lever with your hand. This will sometimes help you realize the feel.

When you can shift in and out of neutral at will, start up the bike and try it again. It will be at least a little bit harder on most bikes and some will seem impossible to find neutral on (we're assuming that the clutch is properly adjusted and otherwise is functioning correctly). Gently rocking the bike forward and back will really help now, although some designs can force you to shut it off to find neutral.

There is a direct correlation between bikes that are hard to find neutral on when the engine is running and bikes that resist starting in gear. That's right, you can start many bikes in gear without having to shift to neutral first. This can be dang handy when you stall it in an awkward situation, such as teetering on the side of a hill. This is a good example of becoming intimate with your bike and learning a simple thing about how she performs, which should lead you to adjust your riding style.

## Lesson 5 - Starting to Ride

It's time to ride! If you're lucky, you'll get a few minutes on a bike with an automatic transmission, which will steepen your learning curve. But no matter, let's go! It is time to start twisting the throttle.

### First Gear Riding

Point the bike in a safe direction on the most open, flat ground available. Even better, if you can take this next step headed down a very slight slope, it will be even easier. Climb aboard with all your riding gear on of course, then stop and talk through what you are going to do. Yup, you'll start her up, grab the clutch and snick her into first. Take a deep breath, dial in a little throttle and use the clutch as you learned in the walking drill to ease the bike into motion, but do not let it out all the way! If the motor starts to die, or the bike starts to move forward more rapidly than you want, immediately pull in the clutch a bit as you learned before. Consider as well, that when you walked the bike under its own power, it was lighter than it is now with your svelte physique aboard. It is going to take a little more throttle to keep the engine from stalling.

If you get the bike to start rolling, immediately stop it by pulling in the clutch and applying the brakes. Do not go more than a few feet. If you are nervous and having trouble getting it to start rolling, duck-walk the bike to help get it moving. Literally, start a slow walk while sitting on the bike as you use your clutch knowledge.

Start and stop, using the clutch only, and do it until you don't have to duck-walk at all, or are at least only giving it one little push off with one foot. You are more in control every step of the way! One day you will get to watch a beginning rider who isn't taught to use the clutch properly first and hopefully you'll only bust a gut laughing and not have to rush over and apply some first aid.

It's time to let the clutch out all the way. Get the bike moving and gradually release it all the way, then immediately pull it in and use both brakes to stop. Practice this a couple times, just to be sure. Never move your hands and fingers from the riding position!

Look at yourself, you can get a motorcycle moving under its own power and stop it without stalling the engine! Okay, you will probably be stalling it here and there until this becomes completely natural, but you know how to find neutral and get her going again, too.

It is okay to start riding around in first now. Keep in mind that once the clutch is all the way out, you are controlling speed with the throttle. In first gear, you'll want to be especially careful to change throttle settings slowly and gently. First is only intended to get you going, or help you through tight or slow and nasty situations. The gear ratio is so low that the engine is capable of overpowering traction easily or accelerating very rapidly, possibly forcing a wheelie if it stays hooked up. Go easy, go slow and keep practicing your stops. Always pull in the clutch when you apply the brakes. If you ever do experience too much throttle, instantly pull in the clutch to gain control of the situation.

Practice gentle turns at first. You are going slowly, so you will tend to have to turn the bars to steer into turns, rather than countersteer. Try some very slow turns using the clutch to creep around them. Put your feet down whenever you feel the need at this point in your career.

## First and Second Gear

Once you have gotten completely comfortable with starting, riding and stopping in first gear, it is time to get out of this relatively useless cog and move to second, where the real fun starts happening.

Okay, you're rolling along in first. Accelerate a bit, so you are away from idle speed and toward the middle-upper portion of the rpm range. Pull in the clutch and roll off the throttle simultaneously. If the clutch is pulled in too quickly the engine will rev up, too slowly and the bike will slow quickly – you'll lose the speed you need for second gear to work properly. In the instant after the clutch is in, shift up firmly. Remember the shifting instructions earlier in this chapter? Okay, lift up on the shift lever with your toe (in the boot, of course) by rotating your heel on the foot peg. Do this firmly and you'll go right past the neutral position between first and second. In the instant after shifting to second, roll the throttle back on while smoothly releasing the clutch. Too slow with the clutch and the motor will rev without accelerating the bike, too little throttle and the motor may bog down, depending on how fast you were going in first.

Yikes! But it's not as complicated as it sounds. Be smooth. Practice the upshift until you get the timing right. It is okay to come to a stop in any gear (pull in the clutch!), then shift back down to first while at a stop.

Shifting down is basically the same but for a couple of points. Where before you wanted to accelerate enough in a lower gear to be going fast enough in the higher gear for the motor to be able to pull the bike, downshifting requires that you have slowed down enough so that when the clutch is released in the lower gear you do not cause the motor to scream and/or attempt to act like a locked rear brake (skid). Always release the clutch slowly on a downshift, paying close attention to the engine. Building revs very quickly - pull the clutch back in and apply the brakes some to slow the bike more before attempting to release the clutch again. If you start to skid, the lower gear you shifted to and the engine's compression are acting as though you applied the rear brake.

It will take the average student a while to get upshifting and downshifting down pat. Practice, be smooth, be patient. Think about how the bike is responding and make adjustments. Go back and forth between first and second until you have it wired!

Turning at higher speeds gives you your first experience with countersteering. Rolling along under power in second, plan to turn. We'll go with a left. Slow slightly entering the turn. Gently push down and forward on the left side of the bars. You will feel the bike lean to the left a bit, go with it. Gently roll the throttle on. Powering, even gently, through any corner always improves the handling of a dirt bike. Experiment carefully with applying more pressure, seeing how the bike leans farther over and turns sharper. Release pressure and see the lean decrease and the arc increase. Until you do it unconsciously, think only of turning by countersteering at any speed higher than a crawl.

## Higher Gears

Shifting up from second on through to fourth, fifth or sixth (whatever your top gear is) and back down uses the same procedure. They're easier because there is more overlap, more forgiveness and more flexibility (what gear you're in vs. speed and throttle position and bike reaction when the clutch is released on a downshift). But you've got to get to second first, so mastering the first-second-first transitions has gotta be done.

Actually, you don't always have to use the clutch at all, especially on upshifts. Simply roll off the throttle, shift and roll it back on. A racer will get so good that they'll hold the throttle wide open and simply upshift, if their bike can handle it. Using the clutch is easier on the machine (except on the clutch itself, of course).

On a downshift, revving the motor up a bit just before the clutch is released will greatly enhance how quickly and easily the motor and rear wheel get in sync for the given gear and speed.

## Counting Gears

Skilled riders always know what gear they're in. A small corner of the brain must be set aside to store the info, for it is a rare dirt bike that has a gear indicator. Riders speak of sections of terrain in relation to specific gears, "That's a third gear section for me," "I take that corner in second," or "You've got to pull third to clear that double" and "Hit the base of the hill in fourth, downshift to third when you get air over the little ledge and drop to second just before the rocks at the top."

Constant awareness of exactly which gear you're in is very useful. It helps you with real time planning in terms of overcoming obstacles, as well as consistency in a track scenario. Why lose a drag race because you're a gear too high, or fail to climb a hill because you didn't realize you were already in first and had no where to shift down to?

Teach yourself to carry the instant knowledge about what gear you're in by "counting shifts." Say the number of the gear you're shifting to as you perform the shift, out loud or at least "loudly" to yourself in your head. As you gain experience you'll find you just know what gear you're in, and with the intimate familiarity you'll acquire about your bike, be able to accurately translate apparent ground speed and engine sound into the answer to, "What gear am I in?"

# Chapter 6

## *YOUR FIRST EXCURSION*

So now you know how to stop your motorcycle, get the engine started, properly use the clutch, shift the transmission and ride around slowly in the lower gears. With this chapter you'll learn how to use more of your motorcycle's capabilities, including some drills to help you quickly refine your skills, and expose you to a variety of concepts which will enhance safety and the joy of riding your dirt bike.

You are ready to go for a ride, keeping in mind the Envelope and the Last Stunt, explained in the very next sections! Keep it simple - avoid steep hills (up or down) and rough, gnarly terrain – the more open the better. You should stay close to support, i.e., your transport vehicle, experienced riders; stay on a route you know or that is well-marked and is relatively free of other ORV traffic. Preferably all of the above.

### The Envelope

The Envelope describes the extent of your abilities, both how much of your motorcycle's capabilities (acceleration, braking, turning, jumping) you can use and the roughness or challenging nature of the terrain you are riding on. As a beginner, your envelope is limited. You hopefully have not taken your motorcycle to top speed or induced maximum acceleration. You have not powerslid through a corner, crested a vertical ledge, gone down a terrifyingly steep hill, or locked up both brakes and pitched it sideways for yards and yards. That is all fine. What is important about the Envelope is how fast you attempt to expand it. If I could stay on your shoulder for the rest of your riding days, this is what I would remind you of. Bite off new chunks a bit at a time, or as I often say, "push the Envelope gently." Master a new expansion of your Envelope before you attempt to expand it more. Oh, so many disasters, even to the conclusion of abandoning the sport, for not heeding this advice. "Wow, I just jumped a 15 foot tabletop and those guys are easily clearing that 50 foot double. I just need to go for it." Wham, bam, thank you ma'am. Go over that 15 foot tabletop dozens of times and you'll scare yourself silly on it soon enough. Work your way up over many rides through bigger and bigger steps before you try to go large. Ditto for any track or trail obstacle and for your bike's performance capabilities.

### The Last Stunt (and the first one)

I can't tell you how many times I or someone I am watching has followed up a great, safe day of riding, maybe even pushing the Envelope gently, by deciding to go for one more lap, one more stunt, one more jump, whereupon a "crash your brains out" incident results. "Tres bummer," as they say. Avoid it.

Ditto the first stunt of the day. Usually this is the first guy in the group to get unloaded, geared up (sometimes stupidly not, "I was just warming her up") and ride. There goes that wham, bam again. Warm yourself up too - take it easy for a mile or three, a lap or three. You're looking for a day of riding bliss, not 90 seconds and a trip to get medical care or parts to fix the steed. One of our AA off-road champions here in the Northwest used to start each race by letting the snarling pros go, banging elbows through the first turn, fighting tooth and nail over the first part of the loop. He'd putt down the start straight, no roost on his goggles, adjusting them and settling into the bike, gradually upping his speed until it was "race pace" and be in the lead by the end of the second lap.

## Lesson 6 – Improving Your Clutch, Braking and Turning Technique

### Donuts

This little exercise will help you fine-tune your clutch/throttle technique, further your understanding of countersteering, and is a fun show-off move for the pit tootsies. Your goal is to ride your bike without going anywhere! Perfectly executed, your bike will spin around in a tight circle, pivoting around your inside foot which barely moves, much like a ballet dancer spinning on a toe. While your rear wheel power-slides around, describing a (drum roll) donut shape, you are using only enough throttle and rear wheel speed to keep it moving.

*Carving a donut, a perfect circle around the pivot foot, demonstrated by NMA AA Champ Kevin Bailey.*

It's easy. Astride your bike in first gear, clutch in, set your left foot on the ground. The donut can be performed with either foot, but it seems to be easier for most to do their first donuts left foot down. Lean the bike to the left and counter-steer to full lock (turn the bars all the way to the right). Roll the throttle on to about 1/3. Release the clutch past the engagement point, but not all the way; control the bike with the clutch!

The leaned-over motorcycle, fully counter-steered, will easily break traction at the rear wheel. The motorcycle will try to move, but everything is set up for a hard left turn, so turn left it will. Keep the throttle steady and control what is going on with the clutch. At first your donuts will tend to be large and jerky, but with a little practice you'll be able to spin tight, consistent, endless donuts, pirouetting on your toe, with it hardly moving from one spot.

The lessons you'll learn about controlling your bike are fully worth nailing this skill. Learn to do them to the right, too. This move will come in handy when you wish to make a snappy u-turn, or one on a narrow trail.

## Figure 8's

This is the best simple exercise. In a very small area it works every basic aspect of riding: clutch, shifting, braking, cornering and throttle. Further, it allows working inside and outside lines in the corners and helps you learn braking distances, or how long you can hold the throttle on before braking hard while still making the corner.

You need a relatively flat, smooth area that allows you to at least accelerate some in second gear, ideally hard in third, which only requires 100-150 feet. The width of the area can be as little as 15 feet, 25-30 feet is plenty. Place a cone or rock or tire or any marker you wouldn't worry too much about hitting or falling on at one end of your area. From a stop at this first marker, accelerate hard down your area. At the point where you would be seriously thinking about shifting to the next higher gear (third if your area is short, fourth if it is longer), pull in the clutch and stop as fast as you can. Set your second corner marker here.

The path you are going to ride is a figure 8 between (around) these two markers, which will give you left and right turn practice. Let's go!

As you ride the figure eight:
- Be smooth. Stand on the pegs once moving on the straights.
- Accelerate and shift up as fast as you are comfortable.
- Brake smoothly, downshifting to first, turning as tight and close to the marker as possible, roll on the throttle as you enter the turn, controlling the bike by countersteering, throttle position and clutch if the motor needs help, all the while weighting the outside footpeg. You are essentially doing half a donut through the turn.
- As you work the figure eight, alternate between inside and outside corner lines, use second gear for the wider line.
- Experiment with braking as late as possible while still making the corner (set up for the inside, fall back on the outside if you brake a tad too late).
- Strive for smooth consistency.

## Lesson 7 – The Standing Riding Position

### Why Stand Up?

Dirt bikes are best controlled from the footpegs, not the seat. I could go into centers of gravity, mass, leverage and reactive vs. proactive and probably bore you to tears. Watch any video of any off-road motorcycling and you will see all the best standing on the pegs when they ride off-road terrain. On trials bikes, where the riding is at the extreme end of the possibilities of controlling a motorcycle over insane terrain, the design essentially prevents riding in a sitting position (you can, but one can't look much sillier than all scrunched up seated on a trials bike). For the longest time trials bike seats were tiny, thin little jokes. These days they don't even bother with a seat and simply put a seat-like sticker there. (Probably because too many buyers would be subconsciously uncomfortable if there was absolutely no seat at all!)

Should I stand up all the time? Well, no, there are plenty of times when it is certainly appropriate to be seated and I'm not just talking just about putting out of the parking area. I've known plenty of pretty fast riders who only stand up in extremely rough terrain or landing from a jump. But all the experts will tell you over and over, you best control a bike from the pegs. Even flat trackers, who look like they are simply sitting all the time, are actually seriously weighting the outside peg through the corners.

It is an excellent idea to put your bike on a stand and try to emulate the following sections, while your guide compares your riding position to the pictures. Get comfortable with this and focus on it as you ride. Make it habitual and natural and you'll go faster, longer, more safely and with better control.

Here's why: the footpegs are located very close to the centers of gravity and mass on the bike. They allow you to use all of the leverage the full length of your body offers, applied right at the most effective point in the system for rider input. The interface between the seat of the bike and your body is not exactly the most functional hunk of muscle you have and likely the least. Through your feet, which you are extremely practiced at balancing on, you respond quicker to balance-impacting inputs. On your butt, your ability to respond is pretty much limited to leaning your upper body and it tends to always be a reaction to something the bike is doing, not pro-active control. On your feet you can move your whole body, not just from the waist up, much farther in every direction. One last point. From the pegs, your body and the bike tend to be unified, leaning and moving together. From the seat, your body and the bike act like they are hinged at that point. In other words, they don't perform in unison. Pro-active and with full control vs. reactive with limited input, your choice.

As soon as you get comfortable with the very basic skills of making the motorcycle stop and go, focus on mastering the standing riding position.

*Multi-time NMA Off-Road champ Kevin Bailey demonstrates the standing riding position – knees slightly bent, chin out over the handlebars.*

### So Stand Up!

The basic riding position is to stand with the balls of your feet (the wide part, just ahead of your arch) on the pegs, knees slightly bent, body leaning slightly

forward so that your chin is approximately above the cross bar of
your handlebars. Gently squeeze the bike between your legs.

## Elbows Out

Standing, leaning forward slightly, grab the handlebars and
position your arms so that your elbows clearly point outward. This
sets up your body to rock with the bike over rough terrain, as well
as so that major muscle groups in your shoulders have the leverage
and are doing the work. A stance with the elbows in tight to the
body forces less potent
muscles in your forearms to
try to handle the load. An
elbows out stance also
improves your angle and
leverage on the clutch and
brake levers. Especially
critical, it allows full rotation
of the throttle (starting from a
slightly "overgrabbed"
position, without scrunching
your whole right side into an
impotent, unreactive, locked-
up twist).

*Bailey, in the standing position
viewed from the front. Notice
the up and out elbows!*

## Hands

This is going to be hard for a while, but don't hang on to the bars
for dear life. You'll just lock up the circulation in your hands and
forearms and no one has enough strength to truly handle the power
of a bike and control the bike against the terrain just by holding on.
That lock up is called arm pump. It will force you to stop and rest
and can actually be painful until you relax.

If you stand properly, grip the bike with your knees, move forward
and backward appropriately and ride with your elbows out, you

will absorb the forces of riding with your whole body and major muscle groups.

In general, grip the bars lightly. Don't think this is black and white. There are moments in the most expert rider's day where a death grip is essential, but there is a near instant return to form. Keep two fingers (fore and middle) extended at all times over the clutch and brake levers. This is called "covering the controls." You may well develop your own comfortable variant of this, perhaps only using one finger on an ultra strong front brake, or a super easy-to-operate hydraulic clutch. Beyond allowing instant response at those critical controls, it leaves your ring and pinkie fingers to wrap around the grip, which you won't be able to squeeze as hard. This will also help prevent throttle accidents, such as when you grab a bit too much and the resultant rearward movement of your body prevents you from releasing and actually rolls on more, increasing the severity of the impending impact.

## The Feel of Guiding Your Bike

Think of guiding your bike through body position, footpeg weighting and a light touch on the bars rather than the notion that you can muscle and force the bike to do what you want. As a beginner or even an average rider, the bike is capable of going anywhere much faster without you aboard (expertly radio controlled), so your task is to guide and facilitate what the bike can do. As an expert rider, your presence and input can make the bike go faster, because you are now enhancing the physics of the situation. For example, proper cornering position applies maximum downforce to the front wheel so that maximum traction, steering accuracy and corner speed are possible.

I'll add one more reinforcement. When I spent a lot of time in the Southern California Badlands in my youth, I used my extensive collection of abandoned orange highway cones to lay out tracks. We play raced on them a lot, but I always practiced alone on them more. Early on, with lap times to back up my seat of the pants feel, I regularly experienced the following scenario. Out I would go, eager as could be, aggressive, ready to attack my track. I was fresh, young, strong and could force my bike to do whatever I wanted, or so it seemed. But at race pace, within a few laps, even if arm pump wasn't setting in I quickly tired, started making mistakes, nearly or completely crashing and certainly getting slower. This was frustrating. So, to keep pounding laps, I would go into cruise mode, relaxed and guiding the bike, not trying to force and muscle it. Dang, within a couple of laps, I was turning faster times than at my best while forcing it and I could run consistently at that pace lap after lap after lap after lap, without major mistakes and staying crash free. It didn't feel as fast as my aggro early laps, but the watch doesn't lie.

Watch the great riders on the tube or in person and you'll see they make it look easy. They go forever. They seem so smooth and effortless. Now you know why. They know no human can muscle and force a bike for long and that such a style is actually slower than riding with finesse.

## When to Lean Forward and Backward

*Accelerating hard across desert terrain on a mighty KX500, Phil Stevens demonstrates getting forward, chin out over the bars, to stay in full control of the bike.*

*Sensing the front of his bike dropping after launching off a kicker jump, Lance Smail hangs his body as far to the rear as he can to counteract the rotation and hit the landing level.*

From the basic standing riding position, you can easily move your body around on the bike in any direction. Most of the time, you will vary from the basic standing position to accomplish a maneuver, sometimes to stave off a crash.

When you're accelerating, leaning forward allows your body to absorb the force down through your legs, otherwise your only way to keep from sliding back is by hanging on to the bars and you now know where that leads. You want to squeeze the bike between your legs instead. This helps you to hold on, further lessening the strength required from your hands and arms.

When you're braking, leaning backwards allows you to absorb the force down through your legs, otherwise your only leverage is once again through your hands. Again, squeezing the bike between your legs helps absorb the forces trying to push you forward on the bike. If you should find yourself forced forward while braking hard, the first bump your rear wheel hits while the rear brake is on will result in the rear of the bike kicking up hard; bad news for sure.

Lean forward while climbing hills. Lean to the rear going down. Squeeze the bike between your legs. Lean rearward over whoop-de-dos.

## When and How to Sit, Cornering Riding Position

Yes, Matilda, the best riders I watch in person or on the tube appear to sit, especially in the corners. What gives? Well, they're not actually sitting. They're pushing on the outside peg so hard that the great majority of their weight is directed there, which is critical to achieving maximum corner speed. It helps drive the side knobs into the dirt.

*A good shot showing proper cornering position. Brian Bennett's butt is all the way forward on the seat. His inside leg is extended, toe up, pointing straight ahead and he is letting the ground "come up" to his foot if/when the bike leans over far enough. His head is forward, eyes focused on the end of the next straight. The elbows are out, two fingers are on the clutch, the throttle is WFO and the rear wheel is roosting. And, he is weighting the outside peg and countersteering.*

While we're here, let's describe the riding position in a corner. Place yourself as far forward on the seat as possible. This maximizes weight on the front wheel. The inside leg is straight forward, knee not locked, toe pointed up and forward. Do not simply put your foot on the ground and try to support the bike. You will hit things with the bottom of your foot with unpleasant results. Extending your leg out like this forces the palms of your hands against the bars, which increases the weight on your front wheel. Never forget, where the front wheel goes, the rear must follow!

Weight the outside peg. You can spot a seat sitter vs. a peg weighter in the corners every time. The seat sitter's bike wallows through the corner. The first surface imperfection or rpm driven power increase causes the rear wheel to kick out farther and the rider can only react with their upper body and by cutting the throttle. The wheel catches as the throttle is cut (if they are countersteering, otherwise the bike spins out), rpms drop and the bike moves back towards the intended line, then the throttle is opened to reverse the speed loss. Through a long corner this wallow cycle may repeat itself several times. The rider can't really begin to accelerate hard out of the corner until the very end of the exit.

A peg weighter carves through the corner. The bike is much more connected to the ground and there is no wallowing. Any more pitching out than intended is fully manageable with more countersteer without having to get out of the throttle.

Lastly, you don't have to sit with weighted peg in the corners. I have seen plenty of experts ride entire motocross courses completely on the pegs. Frankly, riders, even Pros, sit to rest. When the situation is smooth and straight, your bike will do just fine with you fully plopped down and you can relax your legs for a moment. Why not? Keep in mind that constantly switching between standing and sitting is fatiguing in itself, so stay up on the pegs most of the time and sit when you can stay long enough to rest more than what you will lose in energy standing right back up again.

Imagine each corner being based on this sequence. You accelerate as hard and deep as possible while still being able to make a controlled brake to the desired entry speed. You are moving from standing forward and over the front wheel while accelerating, to moving your weight to the rear during the braking. During your braking, your clutch is in and you are counting downshifts to the proper gear. As you release your brakes, you are simultaneously pushing the bars into the appropriate amount of countersteer. Perhaps you drag the rear brake to swing it around a bit, or a lot to "back it in" as they say. At the same time you move down and as far forward as you can, extending your inside toe out and up, fully weighting your outside peg. Also at the same time, (a smooth coordinated set of events indeed) you roll the throttle on and release the clutch out to and beyond the release point. Your head swings up and away from the apex you are going to hit, looking down the next straight. As you approach and pass the apex, you have steadily dialed in more throttle, firmly yet gently powering the bike as it turns best that way, your clutch just barely slipping if at all and you are releasing countersteering pressure and letting her straighten up. Now your extended foot moves back to its peg in anticipation of standing, your throttle finishes reaching wide open and you let the pull slide you rearward to help maximize traction. You stand up and forward, shift up and away you go, grinning like crazy.

## Lesson 8 – Tips

### Mr. Momentum

Mr. Momentum is almost always your friend. He will help you through tough obstacles, get you up hills and make you faster through the corners. Let's start with a simple example, an 18" vertical ledge you must get over. If you put your front wheel against this and try to get over it, you will simply spin your wheel. If you back up fifteen feet and are moving as your front wheel hits the ledge, while standing and leaning back to lighten the front wheel, you can keep the throttle steady and use the clutch to instantly adjust how much power is getting to the rear wheel and you'll crawl right over.

The more speed you can safely carry to the base of a hill and maintain going up, the less likely you will have to use the lowest gears as you climb and wheelspin will be easier to avoid. If it starts spinning, you stop going. Getting moving again after coming to a stop on a significant hill is likely to be impossible.

The higher the gear you're in at any moment, the less likely it is that wheelspin will result from twisting the throttle open. Carry more speed in a corner by using a wider line and that early conservation of momentum will result in a higher speed at the end of the next straight.

Smoothly carrying enough speed to lug third through a boulder field will result in being able to avoid getting stopped hard by the wrong boulder in the wrong place, and the difficulty of getting going again. Consistently use Mr. Momentum, as he will always help you.

## Fixation Phenomenon

The fixation phenomenon is very real. Simply stated, you will go toward exactly what you are looking (or staring) at. If there is a big rock in the trail, you will hit it unless you look to either side of it, where you'd rather go. The alternative, looking where you want to go, is a big part of riding fast. Experienced riders aren't looking at the ground in front of their tire, especially in a turn, they are looking as far ahead as possible and only pulling their focus in enough to make decisions about obstacles along the way. If it is right in front of your tire, you should have made a route decision a while ago, because you *are* going to hit what is there now.

## Getting Stuck On A Hill

If you're attempting to climb a hill and you realize that you are not going to make it, don't simply come to a stop pointing straight up the hill. Things can get ugly real fast from there. Try to imagine riding your bike backwards down a steep hill with the brakes locked up and the tires sliding. (Yes, Matilda, I've done this. Fortunately, it was only about 20 feet back down and I made it. But it took three friends, two tire irons and a large screwdriver to break the suction between a highly puckered orifice and the seat afterwards). As you realize you aren't going to make it, move to turn sideways, across the hill, and as soon as you are perpendicular to the slope stop and jump off to the uphill side of the bike. PLAN AHEAD and act quickly and smoothly. Getting off on the downhill side is even more likely to get uglier faster than trying to stop pointing straight up. From the uphill side, you can control your bike. You can easily push it into facing downhill, grab the front brake, stand it up, get on and roll back down. You can also bulldog it down.

When good riders try to tackle hills they might not make, and as they realize that indeed they won't, you'll often see them pitch the bike around in a turn, or even wheelie up and back around downhill and take off to the bottom in one fluid motion.

## Bulldogging Down A Steep Hill

If you find yourself facing a downhill from a botched climb attempt or simply come across one that is simply too daunting or even too unsafe to attempt to ride down, then bulldog your bike down. Laid sideways across the hill on the uphill side, your bike will pretty much stay put due to having its pegs, bars and other pointy things stuck into the dirt. Scoot down to where your feet, below fully bent knees, are over the middle and rear of the seat and grab the bars normally. Turn them as though you were turning out away from the hill to clear the bar end out of the dirt and push only as firmly as needed on the seat with your boots (your rump stays firmly planted, the bike moves down, you stay put as desired) to move the bike down some.

Once a buddy and I tried to climb all the way up a ridge where the Riverside freeway breaks out of the canyon heading east from Orange County, California. The higher we worked, the thinner and steeper the ridge got and the narrower the trail. All okay, except for the higher we got the harder the wind howled across our path. Soon any slight loss of contact with either wheel and the ground would have the gale moving the offending knobby over a foot, which soon became off the trail. We gave up. Riding down with the wind was terrifying. I was sure one of us was going to endo (going over the bars) and end up rolling down a freaking canyon. So we bulldogged them down, going right over the edge. It was very steep at first, so we jammed the bars back into the dirt along with the boot heels, because once something started moving, everything did. Then it was just steep. We went a couple of hundred feet in all, over all sorts of terrain from little rocky ledges, long sandy stretches where we tried to keep them going in a mini land slide, until we reached the bottom of the canyon – our path to ride the rest of the way out. It works.

# CHAPTER 7

## *GOING RIDING*

### Basic Tips

So you've hooked up with buddies, are going out for the first time with a crew from the shop you snagged an easy invite for, or even signed up alone for a trail ride or a poker run. Here are a few tips.

- Unless fully agreed upon beforehand, you ain't racing. Fall into place in line according to your relative ability. If a pair or more tend to be very equal, you'll naturally swap positions around here and there. If you are new to the group, assume you are the slowest. If there are members who suspect that you are faster than they, you will be encouraged to start out farther up the line. If you misjudge either way, safely move accordingly. If you're being pressed, pull aside for a second and let them pass. If you are pressing, just your presence is enough, you will be let by and no real passing pressure is needed.
- With beginners and youth, good trail ride leaders will take turns bringing up the rear, perhaps riding painfully slow, but certain to be quick to help someone in distress.
- Keep a safe distance between riders according to skill and conditions, especially for visibility. If the person in front stops suddenly, just like on the street the rear-ender is at fault.
- If following on the close side, a part of your awareness should be on the rear tire of the bike in front of you. You will be able to easily spot when the brake is applied.
- If the speed is high, look past the rider in front of you to ensure you see obstacles soon enough to set up for what you need to do to get through. Remember that you are riding the terrain, not the bike in front, so look at what you need to be seeing.
- If it is dusty, you have two choices. One is to literally ride right on the next bike's rear fender, "over and above" their dust. The other and wiser move is to separate sufficiently for the dust to settle or clear. Obviously if you spend much time right in the

thick of the next rider's dust you take vision-related crash risks and your air filter may clog quickly.

- If it is muddy, consider staying back or aside from roost and spray.
- Each rider in a chain is responsible for the rider behind them. This includes waiting at intersections to ensure that the next rider makes the turn and simply verifying that the rider is still making progress along the route.
- If the leader chooses to halt the crew, perhaps at an intersection for a route decision or just for a breather, he must realize that rider sequences almost always progress from the fastest at the front to the slowest at the rear and that those who need it the most will tend to get the least rest. Make allowance for this and you'll have a better ride overall, since thrashing the slowest will only make them go slower as the ride goes on.
- If a rider is injured, never leave them alone. Keep at least one rider with the downed rider and send the others back for help.
- Duh, riding alone is taking a high degree of risk. Riding as a pair only gets more risky if it is a long way to some form of civilization or a long time between other riders coming along. The uninjured rider can't be in two places at once (getting help and staying with the downed rider).

## Trail Etiquette

The following will help keep you safe and also includes tips on how to interact with other types of trail users.

- Upon encountering another group coming toward you on a trail, it is customary for each rider to signal by raised fingers the number of riders still to come in their group. This helps you stay at a slower speed and avoid risking a head on collision, especially in the woods.
- The lead rider in a group and riders in a group that tend to be widely spaced, especially in the woods, must constantly assume that there is a bike coming the other way and be prepared to take evasive action. Broken levers and fingers are common results of such collisions in the woods where speeds are lower. In more high speed terrain, head on collisions can be

very serious. A classic scenario is the hotshot getting way ahead of his group, then turning around and roaring back to find them. I have personally seen maimed bodies and destroyed motorcycles. Don't override your vision!

- When encountering hikers on the trail, do us all a favor and exceed courtesy standards. Stop smoothly and without fanfare. Shut off the engine and attempt to engage in pleasant conversation. Wait until they are fully clear, even down the trail a bit, then take off slowly and quietly.

- When encountering horses, not only pull off the trail and shut down, remove your helmet so the animals can see that you are a human. Follow any instructions the riders request of you. This is the core of what our backcountry equestrian friends ask of us.

- Conflict between different types of users are issues that land managers must, by law, address. The only real solution they seem to have is to shut down trails or shut out a type of user. Since we are the ones being complained about, assume that means you will be shut out. Don't add to our land use and access problems.

# CHAPTER 8

## *CRASHING*

You are going to crash. Here are the four main types of crashes, how they happen and what you might do during one.

### How to Crash

No, I'm not going to tell you how to crash, you'll figure it out soon enough. Show off, exceed your envelope or fail to maintain your bike in safe operating condition and you'll accelerate the process. There are some things you should know about crashing (or almost crashing) though and what you can and should do afterwards.

*The highside crash, performed at the worst possible time - in front of the pack in the first turn.*

First, a tip over is not a crash, no matter how ungainly you make it seem. They only happen when you are going slow, too slow really, and you fail to get a leg out to form a tripod. As you start to tip over beyond recovery, grab the clutch (to possibly avoid killing the motor) and without letting go of the bars, step off and away from the bike. You'll be pushing it back upright before it hits the ground. Not clearing your downside leg will probably result in your bike pinning you to the ground – very ungainly. If your head is downhill/below the bike, you may be very effectively pinned and provide extensive opportunities for your crew to guffaw soundly.

## Low Side, High Side, Looping It and the Endo

There are four basic forms of crashes, one for each direction of your bike's compass: the lowside, the highside, looping it and the endo. For those immediately harrumphing "What about the tank-slapper?" I suggest that it is merely the prelude to a highside, a lowside, or perhaps a highside-endo combo (shudder). For the reader, a tank slapper is the dirt biker's description of a motorcycle that, while generally traveling in the intended direction, has encountered a situation wherein the rear wheel is swinging quite rapidly to the right and left, usually all the way to the steering locks, with each change in rear wheel swing direction initiated by another contact with the ground. Few pull out of this scenario, because one of the rear wheel contact instances usually includes hitting something that initiates a highside. (Double shudder.) Read on.

The lowside often happens in a corner, where the bike gets away from you toward the outside of the corner by completely losing traction at both ends. It slides out from under you. This basically leaves you sitting in the dirt. Try to stay with the bike and keep it running by not letting go of the bars and pulling in the clutch as you go down to save the motor. Generally "no harm, no foul" for your body, these can nonetheless mangle pipes, bend shift or rear brake levers, rip radiator wings off, bend silencers in and other nasty stuff related to sliding your bike along the ground. A lowside can also occur on a straight when a terrain feature or a clumsy piece of input causes the bike to pitch out, but the rider manages to avoid the highside.

The highside usually happens in a corner and is where the bike gets away from you toward the outside of the corner, essentially because both wheels have too much traction. The wheels stick and the top of the bike accelerates toward the outside of the corner like an upside-down pendulum. If you don't release the bars and eject outward, this pendulum effect will pile drive your face into the ground like a swung hammer. If you can let go and fly, the bike's attempt to rotate you into the ground will instead pitch you out like Superman taking off. You will slide when you hit and as long as you aren't letting yourself be pitched into a tree or a wall, you'll come out fine, depending on the speed you were going when it all started.

Generally, highsides happen because the throttle was shut off while the bike was fully into the corner. The rear wheel stops spinning, even slightly (the combination of a tire sliding outward and trying to drive forward under throttle in a corner results in the bike turning) and the tire sticks and stops moving sideways, while inertia keeps the top of the bike moving outward. A highside can also happen on a straight when an obstacle causes the bike to pitch sideways and the rider fails to have the throttle on when it reconnects with the ground. Bike damage in this case is driven by how hard it rotates into the ground. It is more impact rather than sliding damage.

The loop out is when the front wheel gets way up there, even coming backwards over the top of the bike. A wheelie taken way too far would be the basic example. It becomes impossible to stay on the bike. You fall off the back, either bouncing on your butt, somehow landing on your feet (and discovering just how fast you can run) or somewhere between these extremes. Loop outs can also happen while climbing a hill or by poor jumping technique. The bike keeps going and can wad itself up good. If it dances on the rear fender you will probably rip that up, and the silencer, pipe and subframe are all at risk (and expensive to replace). Cartwheeling may also ensue, which can mangle both ends. Or it may roll along a bit and crash to either side, attempting to pretzel the bars and rip things like levers and plastic off the bike.

A loop out because of too much wheelie at low speed or a hillclimbing error might be saveable. Don't let go of the bars and try to stay with the bike. You may end up running along side of it for a few strides before you can swing back on like a cowboy in hot pursuit. If it is a big time loop out, such as getting way too vertical on a jump, bail off by letting go and pushing the bike away. You can buy new bike parts. Healing is a much iffier proposition.

The endo is the most terrifying crash. Basically, your body is headed forward, over the bars and beyond, and the bike is rotating its rear wheel up, over and past the front. Between an obstacle trying to kick the rear wheel up and your weight being too far forward at that instant, or getting pushed in that direction by the kick, over you go. At relatively low speeds this may be where your belly connects with the bars, your butt comes off the seat and your feet off the pegs and you literally kiss the front fender. Done it. Don't let go, try to hold it all straight and you'll likely come out okay.

At higher speeds and levels of kick, you may find yourself in a flying W. This is where you are still gripping the bars, but like a drunken acrobat your feet are waving at the sky. I have seen and personally saved flying W's from proceeding to a spectacular crash, but your underwear is toast and will require changing. In the full endo mode, the bike is rotating forward and over so violently and fast that your only hope is to fly clear, although you will soon learn another rule. A bike, so embarrassed by the endo it must suffer at the hands of the obviously inept rider, tends to hunt down and land on/cartwheel through/roll over the inept rider. Meanwhile, the rider, somewhere in the greatly expanded sense of time between launch and landing, spends at least a few ticks cursing the obviously faulty/ill-designed/mis-valved rear suspension clearly responsible for the predicament. Notably, all single rider off-road vehicles, including quads and snowmobiles, have the same tendency.

Combo crashes result from utterly disastrous mixes of speed, visibility, ineptitude and terrain. Hang around the sport (or watch crash videos) long enough and you'll see them and hopefully avoid the experience. When you do crash, consider these tips:

- Keep your eyes open. Never give up. Where are you going to land, on what, how hard? Continue to identify, decide and act until you stop moving.

- Eject or ride it out (hang on to the bars). From my experience, folks tend to eject too soon, whereas riding it out would have resulted in a near or full save.
- If you're going real fast and you end up sliding on the ground, ride that ride! If you roll over on to your back, you'll be able to keep your arms, legs, feet and hands off the ground – your chest protector makes a nice sled.
- If you eject, tuck and roll just before hitting the ground. Arms extended out in front won't break much of your impact, just your arms or wrists.
- If you took a hard blow, don't be in a hurry to get up. Take stock of your vision, extremities and blood containment system. Yes, if your throttle is stuck in the ground wide open, drag yourself over and hit the kill switch. (I found one once in what amounted to pitch black three dimensional space with no sensation of touch after a brutal third gear lowside on a long bermed right hander when I snagged the peg into the ground. That kill switch was floating out there, but I think it wanted me to find it). Follow the medical professional's instructions, always.

## Inspecting the Bike After a Crash

Don't just jump on your bike after a significant crash and ride off! You may immediately be headed for another biff!

Start with the brakes. Do they seem to work? Pump the lever and pedal. Any sign of fluid leaks? Check your rotors. If bent, the movement forces the calipers open as soon as you start rolling and your next pull of the lever or push of the pedal is likely to go to the stops with no braking action. Prop her up, lay her on the ground, roll her along – whatever it takes – and  inspect the rotors for flatness. If you can't do any of that, test your brakes immediately, at a low speed on safe, open terrain. If the rotors are bent, you'll know it. Each time braking is needed, multiple rapid pumps will result in a reasonable emergency-only braking action which will get you back to the truck.

While you're at it, look over the rest of the controls. Any sign of trouble with the throttle cable? Can you hear the slide plop down in the carb when you release from full on? Operate the steering lock-to-lock. Is the front fender hitting anything? Are the bars bent or not lined up with the front wheel?

Check the exhaust. Look for signs it was pulled away from the engine or pinched shut. Scan the connections between sections and the silencer and look at the mounts. Any sign of any rock punctures to the engine cases? Any sticks or rocks jammed anywhere in the drive train or wheels?

Take off slowly anyway. This will give you time to test everything at a slow pace over safe terrain. If you have any doubts or can't perform adequate trail side repairs, consider not even putting slowly back to camp. Instead, ditch the bike, ride back to camp with a buddy and return with whatever it takes to get your bike going again or out of there.

# CHAPTER 9

## *Basic Setup, Maintenance, Some Simple Repairs, How to Get Her Clean, Some Ideas About Tricking Out Your Ride and Whatever Else Didn't Fit Neatly Into Another Chapter*

## Basic Setup

### Handle Bars

A good rule of thumb for starting bar position is to make them parallel with the forks. Huh? Right. Most handlebars have a smaller diameter tube connecting across the top, called the crossbar. Visualize a line passing between the centers of the cross bar and the main bar and set the bars so that this line is parallel to the forks. To the crossbar, you should mount a crossbar pad, for one day you will kiss this part of your bike hard and it will hurt if there is no pad to absorb your pucker.

Always tighten the forward bolts on the handlebar clamps first, then the rearward bolts. These are critical fasteners, your health considered, so always tighten per the specified torque.

To assess the ergonomics of your bars, you'll need to stand on your bike. Bars come with two basic design variables, height and sweep. If you feel too hunched over or cramped, you might be happier with taller bars. If your hands are bent outward at the wrist, you might wish for less sweep. This is pretty rare on newer bikes. Some newer bikes have reversible handlebar clamps, allowing you to change the basic position.

Bottom line, comfort and control go hand in hand. Your wrists are generally a weak link in the whole bike-body system, meaning if you are not comfortable you will tire fast and have a hard time staying in control.

Bars come in steel and aluminum. There are pros and cons for each, but aluminum designs are most common. There are standard diameters and if you go with something non-standard, you will have to change the mounting system as well.

Not all new bars are cut to length, you may need to get out the hacksaw and cut an equal amount off each end to achieve the desired length. Your physical size might lead you to slightly increase or decrease these basic dimensions, which seem to be common to where one rides. Average seems to be 31 to 31.5", woods riders tend more towards 30" and even as low as 28", and desert rats often prefer a little more leverage and go with 32" or more.

## Levers

For a long time, levers were always set to be at an angle toward the ground, the notion being a clean line down the arms and across the back of your hands in the standing position. Supercross and extreme jumping seemed to be behind the general breakdown of this rule, or maybe it was just a new generation. These days plenty of folks set them horizontal to the ground. I recommend angled down.

There are two things to keep in mind about how fragile levers are when you drop a whole motorcycle on them. You do not want to absolutely clamp the perches (mounts) down. Instead, they should remain loose enough so that a solid whack with your fist will rotate them around the bars. Wrapping the bars with thread (sealant) tape helps them release and rotate under impact.

The second thing is lever width, or how far out on the bars they are mounted. Imagine lines touching the ends of the bars and parallel with the fore-aft centerline of your bike. Position the levers by moving the mounting point of the perch along the bars so that the ball end is never past these parallel lines, throughout the range of operation. This helps prevent snapping off the ends when you drop the bike.

To ensure that only the ball end breaks off if the levers do fail, file a significant notch on the top and bottom of the levers next to the ball. Many come with this notch in place. It will act as a stress riser (focuser). There are also new systems out that are designed to fold back when dropped.

Levers are sometimes, especially with hydraulic systems, adjustable in terms of how far the lever is from the grip and the amount of throw. Make sure you can get your fingers over the lever without letting go. You'll find a set screw with a lock nut to make the adjustment.

For cable-operated systems, the old standard for setting cable tension at the adjuster on the perch is the nickel rule – you should be able to just stick the end of a nickel in the opening between the perch and the lever as all slack is taken up in the cable. The adjuster and lock nut on the perch allow you to change the effective length of the cable's outer sleeve. Also note that there are slots in the adjuster and lock nut. Lining them up with the slot in the perch and lever allows you to remove the cable from the lever, with maximum slack in the system. Do not adjust them such that the slots are lined up for cable removal. Go slightly in either direction for the final setting. Some newer perches have big adjusters that you can operate comfortably while riding.

Bent levers can often be straightened. Take your time and make small adjustments. A vise and a short section of appropriately sized pipe work great. Levers with broken off tips can be used, although it is strongly recommended that you file or grind the end smooth and round to lessen the odds of driving it into your thigh when you crash.

### Shifter

The shifter is adjustable in terms of height. A good starting point is even with the top surface of the footpeg. Variation from that can be driven by foot size, boot style and size (height) and riding position. There is a bolt which pinches the shift lever on the shift shaft. These mate with a splined shaft so you have to completely remove the bolt to remove the shifter. Sometimes a small screwdriver inserted a ways into the slot the bolt pinches shut aids removal. With the bolt removed and the shifter just outside the shaft, adjust position by rotating on the splines. One tooth makes a significant difference. Tighten but don't over-tighten (steel bolt into aluminum) the pinch bolt. There is a channel in the shift shaft that provides clearance for the bolt and prevents total loss should it come loose, but if you don't notice a loose pinch bolt, you're going to strip the splines out of the inside of the shifter. It is a great idea before every ride, if not occasionally during, to give your shifter a little jiggle by hand to ensure it is snug.

Many a bent shifter has been successfully straightened, often on the bike with a big wrench or pliers. Take your time. Correct the problem in small, controlled steps. Consider stopping when it is "good enough" rather than snapping it in two.

*This shifter has been adjusted to be even with the top of the footpeg.*

## Rear Brake

As with the shifter, a good starting place for the height adjustment is even with or slightly below the top of the footpeg. On most bikes there is a bolt and locknut for adjusting. Bending is an option on some designs, typically with steel pedals. On drum style brakes where they are usually operated by a rod between the foot lever and the hub, there is a threaded adjuster, usually a wing nut. The pedal should have a quarter inch or so of movement before the brakes begin to engage.

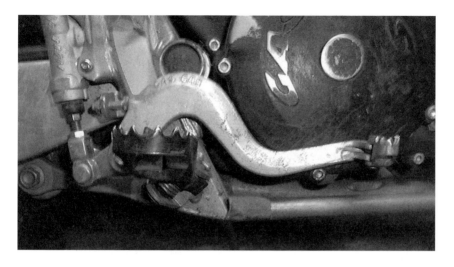

*This brake pedal has been adjusted to be just below the top of the footpeg.*

## Suspension Sag

This is the first thing to set up on your suspension, indeed the most important other than ergonomic stuff. It sets the correct ride height for your weight and achieves front-rear balance, which is essential for good steering and handling and sets the shock to work its best. The golden rule is four inches. That is the difference between two measurements, explained below.

Both measurements are taken between the same two points on the bike, typically (and easily) the bottom of the rear axle and a point approximately straight up on the edge of the rear fender or rear edge of the number plate.

The first measurement is taken with the rear wheel off the ground, either on a stand or balanced on the front wheel and kickstand. The second measurement is taken with the rider standing in the proper position on the pegs, with full riding gear or at least boots and helmet. (I am not saying otherwise naked, by the way, unless you and your tape measure wielding helper are very close.)

*Here is the basic sag measurement being taken. The tape runs from the axle to any chosen point on the bodywork straight above the axle.*

Four inches is the optimal difference between the two. If it is not four inches, you need to adjust the rear shock's spring preload. You'll need a long punch or screwdriver and a hammer. Put the bike up on a stand. It is much easier to adjust with the shock with it unloaded. Find the shock. Near the top are two threaded rings with square slots all around their perimeter. The upper ring is a lock, the bottom the adjuster. Use your punch and hammer to loosen the lock and spin it out of the way.

If your current sag is less than four inches, you need to unload the spring by "unscrewing" the adjuster ring (away from the spring). If it is more than four inches, you need to shorten the effective spring length by tightening the adjuster farther against the spring. One revolution is usually worth about a quarter inch.

Keep your punch or screwdriver placed in the corner of the square slots – take your time, you don't want to round these soft aluminum parts off. Adjust, re-measure and repeat until you get it right. When you achieve four inches of sag, tighten the lock ring, reversing a slot or two worth with the punch.

Some bikes have built-in step adjusters for spring length. Note that four inches is for single shock bikes from about 1980 on. There are shorter suspension travel bikes as well as twin shock bikes where three inches is correct.

**Suspension Dampening**

We could do a whole book on this. Keeping it as simple as possible, suspension response is controlled by spring rate and dampening. Spring rate dictates how much force it takes to move the suspension a given distance. Dampening controls the rate at which suspension moves in response to a given force. A full size modern dirt bike usually has adjusters for compression and rebound dampening for both the shock and the forks.

Compression dampening is a hydraulically-controlled rate of compression of either end of the suspension. Rebound dampening only applies to the extension, or return stroke.

The dampening adjusters are turned with a flat screwdriver (some shock rebound adjusters use a ring). Turning in/clockwise in the tightening direction increases the amount of dampening, out/counter-clockwise reduces it. The adjusters all include easily felt "clicks" at repeated amounts of further rotation of the adjusters (general range of two-to-four clicks per full rotation).

*The shock's compression adjuster is usually on the right side of the bike, at the top of the shock's cylindrical reservoir.*

The compression dampening adjuster for the shock is located at the top of most shocks. The most modern shocks have adjustments for "high" and "low" speed compression dampening. Read your manual. The rebound adjuster is located at the bottom of the shock, often hidden behind linkage arms. It is generally seldom, if ever, adjusted after the initial setting.

The compression adjuster for the forks is typically located at the bottom of each leg, behind a rubber plug. The rebound adjuster is located at the top of each leg. There may also be an air bleed screw at the top of each fork leg.

*Looking up at the bottom of a fork leg, the compression adjuster is visible. It is the slotted screw head in the center.*

These suspension adjusters are spoken of in terms of "clicks" out. The "out" means from fully bottomed, which is screwed all the way in, their maximum compression-dampening setting. Find out where you are set by counting clicks until you can't turn the adjuster in any further – keep in mind that you are working with softer metals here and do not use any significant force or you will damage something. Then simply count clicks back out to return to where you were set. The lower the number of clicks out, the firmer the dampening and the slower the suspension will respond.

Compression adjuster ranges are usually in the 12-24 click range. Start in the middle. If the suspension feels too hard, dial out more clicks, too soft, dial in fewer. Don't stop test riding and adjusting until you have gone too far, then go back. Test with the biggest hits (landing from a jump) and repetitive hits like whoops.

*The fork rebound adjusters are knobs or screws on top of each leg.*

## Tire pressure

The standard starting point for tire pressure is 12 psi. If you are going to be in very rocky terrain, especially at higher speeds, you will help avoid pinched tube flats by bumping up to as high as 15. However, traction will be decreased – beware. In slower going over muddy, rooty, slippery ground, I have known top racers to run as low as 9 psi. Risky, but grippy. Trials bike riders run down in the 3-6 psi range!

## Basic Maintenance

These machines, no matter how well designed and built, even as evolved for their purpose as they have become, are still incredibly abused. Being thrown down, crashed, over-rev'ed, clutch burnt, covered in mud, pelted by rocks, dropped from several stories, buried in dust, submerged and every other possible way of working a machine very hard will take their toll. Your dirt bike might as well go to war. If you don't take care of her, she will let you down. Perhaps you'll only be stranded a jillion miles and two mountain ranges from your truck, or worse, she could fail in a way that causes you physical pain as well as wallet strain.

Dirt bikes have needs. They need to be kept clean, not only for pure pride, but to keep dirt out of moving parts and give you the ability to see damage, loose connectors and the like. They need good fuel and oil and most of all, they need to be caressed by your tools. An experienced rider regularly grabs the wrenches and flows across the entire machine, looking for looseness. They know the state of their air filter, when they last changed the gear oil, how long the piston/rings and/or valve train have gone since their last service. Keep a log book, or set up a chalk, dry erase or grease pen board to help keep track.

A little lesson in mechanical system wear-out will help here. Mechanical systems, like bearings and piston-ring-cylinders, wear like this. There is a quick and minor change in them as they break in. Minor imperfections are being quickly ground away. Then they operate as planned, wearing slowly. At some point along the way, the amount of wear becomes enough that the increasing gaps serve to accelerate the pace of wear accumulation. They essentially reach a point where instead of normal, gradual wear, they actually eat themselves up. So unless you're a factory star and essentially get a brand new bike (via complete teardown and rebuild every race), you need to do maintenance on mechanical systems before normal wear starts to accelerate, because that is when the repair bills start to accelerate in size as well.

Here are a few maintenance tips and instructions.

### Fuel

Think fresh, think premium. You don't need race gas unless you have a highly-tweaked race motor and then you may be fine with a 50-50 mix. Buy from a station that gets lots of business and turns over their inventory regularly. Try to buy from the same station or chain always. There are plenty of seemingly true accounts of race bikes having a jetting sensitivity vs. brand. Use a clean gas can certified for that job.

NEVER fill a gas can while it is in the bed of your pickup, especially a plastic can, or even metal if you have a plastic or coating-type bed liner. Flowing gas actually builds up a static charge that will jump from the opening to metal if it can. That resultant spark will ignite the fumes and you can imagine the rest.

If your gas gets old, use it in the lawnmower or the car. Drain your bike's tank and float bowl if you let it sit for more than a couple of months. A stored bike seems to do best with an empty carb and a tank full to the brim (or bone dry).

Your four stroke, or oil injected two stroke, simply needs straight gas. Your two stroke needs an appropriate oil mixed with it.

**Air Filter**
Keeping your filter clean and oiled is vital to the life and performance of your engine. If you ride in dry, dusty conditions, you need to clean it every day, perhaps even sooner. I have seen plenty of races where an engine can be ruined in less than three hours (savvy crews have clean and oiled filters ready for a quick change). Once a filter is completely coated with dust and dirt, it will start pulling the debris into the engine, if the engine will even run!

To get at your filter, you'll have to remove a side panel (number plate or access door) and/or the seat. Unless you're in a great hurry, best to remove everything associated with access and visibility. You'll do a better job. By the way, dirt bike air filter maintenance is the best single reason for buying a box of rubber gloves at the auto parts store. It is a messy, sticky job. Besides, you'll have lots of fun with the jokes as you slip them on.

There is a single long bolt (wing nut style) or a clip holding the filter in place. Remove it. Carefully lift the filter (there is a plastic cage underneath it) away and out. Try not to let any dirt get knocked off and into the intake boot!

There are many ways folks clean filters: liquid laundry soap and hot water in the sink, in the washing machine on the gentle cycle, pouring gas through it or dipping and squeezing it in a tub of gas. You can buy filter cleaner chemicals at your shop which dissolve the dirt. Bottom line – get it completely clean, inside and out, without stressing the glued seams in the foam (i.e., be relatively gentle as you wring it out and avoid the solvent tank).

Then, you MUST oil your filter (you're appreciating those gloves now, I'll bet). Optimum is a filter oil made for the job. In a pinch, use the same oil you mix with your gas. The combination of the foam and oil is what it takes to really trap all the dirt. Whether you spray it on or pour it in, work the oil gently throughout the entire filter, gently squeezing out any excess. A plastic baggy helps with the pour method, and of course another entrepreneur came up with a special tub for the job. Either is a great place to store a spare filter.

Clean off the cage and inspect the inside of the intake boot. If there is dirt in there, get it all out. If the filter was not hopelessly dirty and you didn't knock any there during removal, find and fix the problem (likely a filter failure, probably at the area where the mounting bolt goes). If there was a lot of dirt, you are going to have to remove and clean the carburetor as well.

Finally, apply a decent film of waterproof grease around the interface between the filter and the airbox. Some filters have a shaped mating surface, making it easy to apply the grease. Otherwise, apply the film to the mating surface on the airbox, but don't glob it around so that any can be easily sucked into the carb. Your goal is to create a film to help seal the filter-seat interface.

Place the filter over the cage. There are alignment features which must be used. Carefully slip the filter into place (glad you took the seat off, too, eh?), make sure the cage alignment feature (typically a pin into a hole) is correct to the airbox and hand tighten only the bolt or slip the clip into place. Inspect everything twice. Notice how it was easier to do a great job on this critical task with both the side panel and the seat off?

## Spark Plug

In general, you will spend more time with your spark plug in a two stroke than a four stroke engine. Even perfectly jetted, a two stroke is harder on the plug. All plugs will fail eventually – there are books on this subject alone. The following covers only the critical points.

Some bike plugs take a special configuration plug wrench, while some can be wrenched with the same tools used on your truck. Many four strokes require an extra long socket, usually supplied with the bike. These cheap stampings work, just use a screwdriver through the supplied holes rather than a wrench on the loosely defined hex and they'll last, too. Many two strokes need a very short height wrench or socket-like tool.

If your bike isn't starting or running right and you want to check your plug, start by removing the spark plug wire. Be gentle, you don't want to damage the wire-cap interface! With the correct tool, remove the plug as with any normally threaded bolt (counter clockwise).

To test a plug, I recommend using one line in a set of jumper cables to ground it. Attach one clamp to an unpainted bolt on the engine or the engine mounts. Attach the other to the hex part of the plug the wrench interfaces with (the outside metal body of the plug). Kick or turn the engine over, examining the "gap" between the center electrode and the arm which is part of the threaded outer body. Anything but a big, fat, blue, regular spark and you've got a problem. A weak, yellow spark will probably not spark at all inside the higher pressure cylinder. Test with a new plug and if this fixes it you're on your way. If you can't utilize a jumper cable or a wire with an alligator clip at either end, it does work to hold the plug against the cylinder head. Be aware that you are risking a jolt should the problem involve the plug wire and I have seen one bike catch fire. (It was very flooded and when kicked over to check the spark, the plume of fuel ignited. Got it out about the same time it flamed out. Yeah, I did that one in my early teen years.)

Do not over- tighten when installing a plug! You are putting steel threads into an aluminum cylinder head; that will be an expensive fix. Firm but not too tight! And plugs have a "gap," the distance between the center electrode and the ground arm. Check your new ones!

Plugs come in different heat ranges. The lower the number, the hotter the plug. Run what is recommended for your bike - do not go to a hotter or colder plug without consulting an experienced mechanic. Some bikes' modern, computerized ignitions require very specific resistance value plugs. Also know that plugs come in different "reach," which is to say how long the threaded portion of the plug is. Since you will bottom the base of the threads against the cylinder head, the reach must be exact for your engine – too long and the piston will bounce off the plug, too short and it will be hidden up the hole, messing up ignition at the precise instant of combustion. For a great many years and still, most two stroke bikes, 125 and 250 on up to 500 and even many 80s and 100s, all used the same reach plug - certainly convenient.

I am not going to go into "plug reading" in the detail that books have been written to cover. At the simplest level, if the area around your plug's center electrode is black, gooey even, it is fouled and your engine is jetted rich, or you have more serious maintenance issues. A new plug may solve the problem, for a while. If it is stark white, your engine is lean and will soon become "one piece." If it is tan or gray, everything is fine. Carrying a spare plug and the needed tool with you on any ride more than a couple miles from camp is wise.

## Chain Adjustment

The chain is a pretty critical part of your bike. Elsewhere in this book you've read about types of chains and how to lubricate them. This section will describe adjusting it and when to replace it. An old or misadjusted chain robs power and can be dangerous if it has reached the point where it comes off the sprocket easily.

Adjusting a chain can be done with the rear wheel on the ground, but it is easier with the bike on a stand. You'll need a big wrench for the axle nut and pliers to remove the cotter pin, if so equipped. On bikes that don't use a simple cam system to adjust rear axle position, you'll need wrenches for the adjuster nut or bolt (typically 10, 12 or 13mm) and for the lock nuts, if so equipped (12mm). Most bikes employ an axle that locks into a non-rotating position at the "bolt" end. If not, you'll need a wrench for that side (opposite the axle nut).

Remove the cotter pin by straightening and aligning the legs and pulling it out. These can get quite mangled, but vise grips can help. A cotter pin may simply go through a hole in a bolt and be there to stop a nut from getting more than loose. The more sophisticated design sets that hole to correspond to an opposite pair of notches in a castle nut and prevent all but the slightest movement of the nut.

Loosen the axle nut until the outer face of the nut is a bit past the end of the axle. Tap on the outer face of the nut (you've protected the axle's threads by that nut placement) to move the axle slightly through the hub so that it is clearly loose on both sides.

If you have cam-type adjusters, rotate them to achieve the correct chain tension (see below). It is a rare day that a chain is being loosened; to tighten up a loose chain you are going to move the axle rearward on the bike. That will be toward a bigger number on the cam.  For threaded adjusters, hold the adjuster in place with its wrench and loosen the lock nuts if present. Assuming that your rear wheel is already aligned (see below), count flats. Flats are the hex surfaces your wrench touches. Moving the adjusters on both sides of the bike the same number of flats ensures that alignment is maintained.

To check adjustment progress, load up the system to pull the axle hard against the adjusters. Do this by placing an average size screwdriver across the rear sprocket, in a groove between two teeth and rotating the wheel to trap the tool between the chain and the sprocket. Don't overdo it, you will see how this pulls the system tight and snug.

Your manual provides a torque for the axle nut and a torque wrench is the proper way to go, but you will adjust your chain a jillion times without a torque wrench and be fine. Clamp it down hard. If it uses a cotter pin, of course you have to line up the slot in the castle nut and one of the holes in the axle, in conjunction with achieving tight. It is best, considering how the legs of the cotter pin will be bent vs. how they will hit dirt, to insert it from the top or rear. Use a fresh cotter pin unless the old one looks great.

*A typical chain adjuster assembly. Turning the nut on the threaded rod moves the position of the rear axle in the slots in the swingarm. The alignment gauge are the notches in the swingarm above and below the axle and the round bumps on the adjuster, again above and below the axle.*

Holding the adjusters with their wrench, tighten the lock nuts firmly.

## Re-check Chain Tension

What is the proper tension? Most people adjust them too tight and the chains will stretch under the resultant load and constantly need adjusting. All chains break in a bit (stretch) at first, but then they should settle down and not need constant adjustment, especially o-ring chains.

The longest a chain needs to be occurs at the point in suspension travel where the centers of the countershaft sprocket, swingarm pivot and rear sprocket are on a line. At any other point in suspension travel, the rear sprocket has rotated closer to the front via the swingarm pivot and the chain will have more slack.

Few if any bikes have these points in a line with the wheel hanging off the ground. With them aligned, the chain should be approaching tension, but there should still be some play up and down in the middle of the run between sprockets. Or better yet, you should be able to pull the chain back away from the rear sprocket a little bit. The links should not be under tension at all. Then with the wheel hanging, this will typically equate to being able to easily slip three fingers between the chain and the rear of the upper rubbing block on top of the swingarm a few inches back from the swingarm pivot (the measurement point is about midway between the two sprockets). You could disconnect your shock, line everything up, set the chain, put it all together and see where it comes out when everything is not aligned, or get someone to sit on the bike and compress the suspension to align everything and then check it hanging to calibrate the system to your bike.

## Chain Replacement

If you can pull your chain off the rear of the rear sprocket a quarter inch or more after it is otherwise properly adjusted, you probably need a new chain.

If the teeth on either sprocket are "hooked" significantly, or getting thin and sharp, you probably need a new chain (and sprockets).

If you can easily feel looseness from plate-to-plate, roller pin-to-roller pin… you get the message.

If your adjusters are getting close to their maximum and you don't have more links in your chain than the stock number, it is time.

If you remove the chain and attempt to hold it so it supports itself (plates parallel to the ground) and the other end points straight down (rather than out and away from you), ditto.

You can buy chain at exactly the right link count for your bike, or buy a chain breaker and cut your own. It is wise to replace the sprockets if they are worn, for they will significantly shorten the life of your new chain. Popping for steel rear sprockets (aluminum is typical stock) will have you rarely if ever replacing them. Replacing the rear sprocket requires removing the rear wheel, unbolting the old one, cleaning up all mating surfaces and installing the new one. Replacing the front sprocket requires removing any covers in place and unbolting a retainer plate or removing a circlip.

It is easy to string new chain on a dirt bike. You can always pull the new chain through a well-covered countershaft sprocket by connecting the new to the old (before it is off) with the master link (just the half with the pins, temporarily).

To remove the clip on the master link, rotate the chain so that the clip is on the top rear of the rear sprocket, which will help hold things in place for you. Place a flat screwdriver against the open ends of the clip. A light knock with your palm on the handle of the screwdriver is usually enough to pop the clip forward off the pins without it flying away; of course keep your thumb over it. There is a larger hole in the center of the clip. It will now be over the forward pin. Rotate the clip around the pin and lift it off. Use the flat blade to gently pry the outer plate off the master link and push the part of the master link with the pins out.

It can be instructive to lay your old and new chains on clean cement side-by-side. You'll be amazed at the stretch in the old one.

Reverse the master link disassembly to put the new one on. The plate and clip always go on the outside of the sprocket (away from the hub). It is absolutely critical that the closed end of the clip face forward relative to the direction the chain travels when the bike is rolling forward, else you risk catching the open ends of the clip and losing it, with disastrous results. Set the hole in the clip over the forward pin of the master link, rotate it to line up with the rear pin and use the same flat blade screwdriver/palm of the hand thump to pop into position. That position is where the clip is clearly seated in the grooves in the outer ends of the pins.

O-ring master links are a bear to install. One method uses two pairs of vise grips to work the outer plate of the master link over the pins and compress the o-rings enough to expose the grooves in the ends of the pins for the clip. A C-clamp, or vise grips, with a suitable nut for the pin to extend into also works. Save your old master link for an emergency need.

On full size bikes (125cc and above) with 520 or bigger chain, you can usually switch from non-o-ring to o-ring. The only hang-up to be modified might be at the width of the chain guide. On small bikes, the switch usually requires thicker sprockets as well.

*The case saver is the curved aluminum bar directly to the left of the countershaft sprocket and chain.*

One last tip. The worst thing a failed chain can do to your bike is to break and, as it will probably do it under power, the countershaft sprocket will attempt to wad up and drive the chain through your engine cases, costing you a small fortune to replace. Ask at your shop for a "case saver." This bolts on in place of (sometimes with) the countershaft sprocket cover. It is in the form of a curved bar, the width corresponding to and aligned with the rollers in the center of the chain. Its job is to channel a broken but still being pulled chain down and away from where it can wad up between the cases and the sprocket.

## Tires

These are actually the most important part of your bike in terms of performance. Forward motion, braking, cornering and nearly all aspects of controlling your bike are all compromised with heavily worn or the wrong tires.

Across the various manufacturers you can expect to find an array of designs based on soil conditions typically called soft, intermediate and hard terrain. If you ride in sand, mud, loose loam, roots and ruts, choose a soft terrain design. The knobs are small in surface area and widely spaced, with the center knobs simulating a paddle design. These will wear very fast, even chunk or throw knobs, if run aggressively on rocky or hardpack terrain.

Intermediate tires attempt to do a decent job everywhere and are typical OEM equipment. They are probably the best choice for most riders.

Hard terrain tires are aimed at rocky or hard packed terrain. They wear like iron and tend to handle like it too.

You will be surprised at the extent of the handling and performance differences between worn and new tires. After your front tires see their knobs rounding off, cornering precision, traction and braking power will decrease. The rear knobs are not quite as sensitive to a little rounding, but they wear out approximately two-to-three times faster than the fronts.

Some tires are reversible. If the design is rotation direction specific, it will clearly say so on the sidewall.

Stick with the sizes that came on your bike. For most full size dirt bikes, a 21 inch front wheel is standard (20" wheel fads come and go) and the Japanese bikes tend to come with 19" rears, the European with 18". Methods of depicting tire width and sidewall height can vary between manufacturers, unfortunately. In general, the numbering system will be XXX/YYY – ZZ. XXX indicates the width of the tire in metric dimensions. YYY indicates the height of the tire as a percentage of the width. ZZ indicates the diameter wheel the tire is intended for.

**Tire Replacement**
Below is a step-by-step process for changing a tire, including some tips the ISDE (International Six Days Enduro) guys use.

- Remove the wheel from the bike. Ensure that you know how all spacers and fasteners go and place them on the axle as they were on the bike to help you remember.
- Loosen the rimlock nut all the way to the end of the threaded shaft, but do not remove.

- Remove the valve core. If the tire is still pressurized, either deflate it first by pressing the little button on the valve core, or be prepared to deal with it trying to shoot out. Most auto parts stores sell a nifty tool which includes the extractor and taps to clean up threads. There are also metal valve stem caps with an extractor built in – it is recommended that at least one of your wheels has one. Some tubes come with an extractor built into the plastic cap, although these seem to work once if at all.
- Break the beads on both sides of the tire free before starting to dismount it. Use your boot and step down hard on the side of the tire, with the disk brake rotor up (not against the ground). To "break the bead" means to push the inner part of the tire that interfaces and seals up against the outer wall of the rim into the center area of the rim. Do the other side too, by hand; it will be easy and not stress the rotor.
- Remove any nuts from the valve stem.
- Grind a 1/16" deep groove across the width of your basic tire irons (forget the screwdrivers), half an inch from the flat, rounded end (the why comes in a few sentences).
- Start with the disk brake rotor up (sprocket down for the rear).
- Begin at the rimlock – use it to protect your tube. Push the rimlock stud to move it into the tire slightly. Insert the hooked ends of two tire irons at either end of the internal part of the rimlock until the hook engages the edge of the tire's bead.
- Press the bead of the tire, opposite the rimlock, down into the center of the rim and hold it there with your knees and lever the tire irons so as to lift that section out of the wheel. You can set the end of one iron carefully under the rotor to hold it there.
- With the rounded end of a third tire iron, work your way around the tire. Slightly relaxing the adjacent tire iron can help at first. This should not be needed after you're almost a quarter of the way around. You can go all the way around in one direction or alternate instead. The first two irons will not be needed after half of the tire is outside the wheel.
- Remember, it is a lot easier if the portion of the tire's circumference opposite where you are levering the iron is down into the center of the wheel any time you are levering the beads in or out of the wheel.

- Flip the wheel over and do the other side. Really. Don't struggle with removing both beads off the same side of the wheel. This is how the ISDE guys do it (including the next bullet) and they have precious few minutes to work on their bikes each day.

*This shot shows the tire iron in place ready to lever another section of tire out of the rim.*

- When both beads are outside of the wheel, stand it up. The wheel will drop down into the tire and be clear of the beads at the top. It is quite easy now to peel the tire sideways off the top of the wheel and lift the wheel out.
- Now to install the new tube and/or tire. Note: cold rubber resists the flexing needed to remove or install. Let the sun, or some time inside by the heater, warm things up to make it all easier.
- You don't need a new tube every time. I have used them for years. Do watch for rust at the valve stem. Tubes that don't fail due to puncture eventually die around the stem. Of course, lack of a rimlock will rip a valve stem out every time, as the tire and wheel will not stay rotationally aligned with the low pressures we need.

- Slightly inflate the tube, so that it just holds shape but is not expanded. I still baby powder mine – it cuts friction and galling between the tube and tire. Insert all of the tube except 6-8 inches, with the valve stem in the center of that into the tire. Trick: in an emergency, a front tube will suffice in the rear (the opposite is not possible).

*When both sides of the tire are outside of the rim, the rim will tend to fall down into the tire. You can see the tire being peeled off the rim here. Get it part way off and the rim will easily lift straight out.*

- Examine the old tire and wheel. If it went flat, you must learn why or it will probably immediately go flat again – the culprit is still there. A loose spoke is a real possibility. Feel around the inside of the tire for something sharp that has punctured it and stayed in the rubber. Sometimes, a wicked impact against a sharp rock with our low pressures will pinch the tube. This is easy to spot as a short cut or a matching pair of cuts across the width of the tube. Once a tube has been punctured, only use it patched for the shortest time possible. Yes, I have seen patched tubes last a long time, but tubes are cheap and flats suck.

- If you have broken or bent spokes, replace them.
- There is a rubber strip around the inside of the wheel that protects the tube from the spoke nipples. Duct tape can be used as a replacement (in this case it is called "100 mph tape"), just be sure to use at least two, preferably three, layers. I prefer this to be under the rimlock. You'll have to cut a hole for that and for the valve stem.
- I don't find it necessary any more, but lubricating the tire's beads with baby powder, soapy water, or even a spray lubricant is popular. I think it just makes a big mess. Good technique and tools really negate the need.
- Stand the tire-tube assembly up vertically with the stem at the bottom of the circle pointing up. Set the wheel's tube hole over the stem, immediately installing the nut. (Hondas haven't used a nut in a while; instead, they have this rubber gizmo. Install it!) Shove the last of the tube into the tire and one side of the bead inside the wheel. Do this so that you are putting the bead into the wheel on the opposite side from the sprocket. Lay the tire flat (sprocket side down). You should be able to force half or more of the bead over the wheel by hand, using your knee to keep the inserted bead down in the center well of the wheel.
- Now it is time for an iron. One of the longer ones with an arc'ed end is ideal. The iron is placed under the bead so that the arc wraps around both beads (push any exposed tube inside). Levering this iron easily rolls the first bead over the rim. You will be finishing at the rimlock, since you started at the valve stem. For balancing purposes, they tend to be opposites.

*Note the position of the curved end of my favorite tire iron as the last part of the first bead is leveraged over the rim.*

- Push the rimlock in, (the nut will keep it from going all the way in), then use your flat irons to lift the bead over it to the other side.
- Now to get the last bead in. This is where most novices pinch their tube and have to do it all over again. The grooves you ground in your tire irons will really help you here. You can get the process started by hand again, so work as much of this last side over as possible. When you resort to the irons, insert them with the groove against the rim. You want the groove to be at the edge of the wheel's rim. You can feel it click into place. The groove is to be used as the fulcrum of the iron as you lever it and it prevents over-insertion of the iron, which is what will catch and pinch your tube. When you get to the rimlock, push it into the tire before popping the last of the bead in.
- Voilà! You're almost done! Make sure that the tire and wheel are aligned rotationally, so that the valve stem shoots straight out of its hole and is not under stress. You can adjust the

alignment easily, just gab the spokes and the tire and give them a jerk.

*You can see the iron as it has just levered one of the last sections of the second bead into the rim. Notice how little of the iron is inserted. There is a groove in this iron to control that.*

- Inflate the tire until the beads seat. I did this forever with a simple plastic tube bicycle pump, calling it a workout. I have used a 12 volt emergency tire inflator. Compressed air is fastest. Sometimes the rimlock will fight bead setting. If so, all you can do is deflate or perhaps add a little lubricant to that zone and try again. Do not inflate more than required.
- While you are over-inflated, listen for leaks.
- Deflate the tire to the pressure you wish to run. Tighten the rimlock down good and be sure to remove the valve stem nut. You are less likely to tear the stem out of the tube if there is some play in the system.

## Spokes

When a bike is new, the spokes will loosen up. (Best to check them before you even ride it. They can go south in a hurry.) It is best to buy a spoke wrench, since their special design prevents rounding the relatively soft flats on the spoke nipples. The spoke nipples are located at the outer, rim end of the spokes.

The following test is sound, unless your tool box is so trick that it is home to a torque spoke wrench. Lightly rap the spoke wrench against each one. Loose ones will reply with a dull thud, tight ones with a sustained ringing tone. Variations in tightness vary the tone, just like tuning a guitar. Picture screwing the spoke nipple at the wheel onto the spoke to tighten them. The spokes are different lengths front vs. rear and often side-to-side. Don't try to tighten them all to the same pitch, only do that within each side of each wheel.

Go slowly, making small adjustments, working your way all around the wheel. Expect looseness on either side of the rimlock. If during adjustment on an older bike, you encounter frozen nipples (brrrr), apply an oil like Liquid Wrench or Marvel Mystery Oil and let it soak lest you destroy the nipple. Another tip: break a frozen nipple free by first loosening the spoke rather than tightening it and then gently go back and forth between each direction. You'll be rewarded with happy, loose nipples.

In almost all cases they seat and tend to stay put after a few rides and spoke checks. A brutal, fast, hard ride or many big jumps and impacts can loosen them up. Part of your pre-ride check should include a look at the spokes, but testing them with tire change intervals after break-in might suffice.

## Brake Adjustment

As these are the most important part of any vehicle, you'd be wise indeed to maintain them. There are several areas which might need your attention.

We'll start with how to adjust your brakes, as that knowledge is needed both on an ongoing basis and after any parts are replaced or serviced. There is a rule of thumb for adjusting any lever movement called the nickel rule, which suggests that the ideal free play, or amount the lever has to be moved before anything starts happening, is equal to the width of a nickel. The same is true for pedal (rear brake) adjustment. Lack of free play in a brake system means that the brakes are always actuated to some extent, negatively impacting performance and wear. Too much free play reduces or limits the total braking power available.

After making any adjustment or performing any service always verify that each wheel spins freely (yes, the rear less so due to the chain), with zero or only minute drag from the brakes when off and that the brakes easily stop a spinning wheel when actuated.

Hydraulic disc brakes can only be adjusted in terms of how the lever or pedal actuates the master cylinder, assuming the fluid itself doesn't need service. For the front brake, the lever has a threaded adjuster which interacts with the piston in the master cylinder. This should be adjusted so that there is a bit of play, meaning that the first little movement of the lever only accomplishes taking up the play, after which further movement starts to work the master cylinder. There may also be a threaded adjuster which sets the position of the lever relative to the bars. It operates between the perch and the lever. For the rear brake, there is a threaded adjuster which sets pedal position and where the pedal interacts with the master cylinder, mounted directly aft and above the rear of the pedal. There may also be a threaded adjustment regulating the free play, or how much the pedal moves before starting to actuate the piston.

Drum brakes are mechanically actuated. For the front brake, a cable is used. There is almost always a threaded adjuster at the perch. The function of this adjuster is to change the effective length of the tube the cable passes through. Shortening the tube by turning this adjuster into the perch will create more play. The lever will have to be moved further before cable slack is taken up and the brake begins to actuate. Lengthening the tube by turning the adjuster out of the perch takes up cable slack. Sometimes there is an additional adjuster near the brake drum, working by the same logic.

Cable-operated rear brakes have the same adjustment methods. Most rear drum brakes are rod actuated, though. The rod is threaded where the rod connects to the arm at the drum and a wing nut, which can easily be turned without tools, is provided. It helps to move the actuating arm away from the wing nut, but it is not necessary. The wing nut has a curved base which prevents it from self-adjusting. There is another adjustment that may be possible with drum brakes, although it must be understood that this is useful only with very worn brake shoes. That is to move the actuating arm one "tooth" on the serrated shaft it is mounted to.

## Brake Pad/Shoe Replacement

Disc brakes use pads, drum brakes use shoes. The material which actually contacts the rotor (pads) or the inside of the drum (shoes) will wear out. If the wearable material is completely worn away, then the metal foundation of the pads or shoes will directly contact the rotor or drum and immediately start to damage it, quickly ruining it. Replacing a rotor is expensive but not too hard to do, whereas replacing a drum is expensive and involves complete disassembly of all of the wheel's spokes.

On dirt bikes, disc brakes are hydraulically actuated. Hydraulic pressure in a master cylinder created by operating the lever or pedal is transmitted via hose to a slave cylinder in the caliper at the wheel, where a piston is then pushed out which in turn presses and clamps the pads against the side of the rotor. Drum brakes are cable or rod actuated. Actuation of the lever or pedal is transmitted to an arm at the drum and movement of the arm rotates its "axle." Inside the drum, this axle is shaped as a cam. One end of each shoe lays against this cam and rotating it forces the shoes apart and against the inside of the drum.

Pads are easy to inspect. Simply look into the caliper and see how much wearable material the pads have left. Shoes generally require removal of the wheel to inspect. Some manufacturers provide a rudimentary wear gage at the arm actuating the cam which spreads the shoes to accomplish braking action.

Pads (and sometimes shoes) are available in more than one material. Softer materials provide stronger braking action but wear faster, while harder materials do the opposite.

Pads are very easy to exchange. The caliper must be separated from the rotor. There are two methods: remove the wheel or remove the caliper. The pads are trapped in place by pins (about a quarter inch in diameter), which are threaded in place and usually require an Allen wrench to remove/replace. There may be covers over the Allen head to help keep dirt out. You will need to depress the piston, which looks like an open cup, fully into the caliper in order for the new, thick pads to fit over the rotor. Remove the master cylinder cover (front brake) or reservoir cap (rear brake), as fluid will be forced back up into the system. If you have been topping off the master cylinder or its reservoir, you will need to spoon out some of the fluid or it will overflow. You can often force the piston into the caliper by hand, or use a tool such as a C-clamp. Go very slowly! Do not use any tool in any way that will mar or damage the edge of the cup shaped piston. Clean and lightly lube the pins, replacing them if they are damaged. It is important that the pads move freely along the pins. Never get any oil or lube on the pad or rotor surfaces. Use brake cleaner, available at any auto parts store, to thoroughly clean the pads if you do. Be prepared to replace pads in one uninterrupted work session and you will be more likely to remember exactly how they go in. Do not ride the bike if you have any doubts about your brakes.

Shoes are easier to replace. You will have to remove the wheel to access them. You will also need to completely back off all adjusters to "make room" for the new shoes. The shoes are held in place against the cam and the upper pivot point by springs which stretch between the shoes. Study yours closely before you disassemble them and put the new ones on accordingly. A helpful hint is to, after connecting the springs, lay the shoes against each other, side-to-side and then "unfold" them over the pivot pin and cam. This is much easier than attempting to spread them apart by muscle power.

### Brake Fluid

Brake fluid is a hydraulic fluid intended to survive the high local temperatures brakes can create. Brake fluid is rated as "DOT" plus a number. It is best to use what the manufacturer recommends – it is often labeled on the reservoir, but expect to use DOT 4. Three is okay in an emergency and I have seen 3-4.

Brake fluid wears out. It gets dirty and the stuff is very hygroscopic, meaning it strives to absorb water, which ruins brake fluid. It is also possible to get air bubbles in the system, further degrading performance (mushy, weak response) and possibly causing the brakes to stop working entirely. It is a good idea to replace stock fluid with a higher quality product shortly after getting the bike. If you purchased a used bike, I strongly recommend replacing the fluid ASAP. Then make it part of your regular inspection and maintenance. You *do* want your brakes to always work to the best of their capability.

With windows or clear reservoirs, all dirt bike disk brake systems make it very easy to check brake fluid clarity and level. If it is getting dirty (or burnt, which also darkens it), that will be obvious. If it is cloudy, it has water in it. If the level is low, that is obvious.

The front brake has a single reservoir, located at the lever's perch. There is a window in the box-shaped reservoir. The reservoir is replenished by removing the top cap. There is a rubber bladder/seal underneath. Be careful with it. Use the right fluid for your bike! The wrong stuff can destroy all of the rubber seals throughout the system, almost instantly.

The rear brake has a reservoir with a screw-on cap. It is a little clear bottle, usually located on the right side of the bike near the carb or behind the radiator wing. Brand new designs are integrating this reservoir with the rear master cylinder.

*The rear brake reservoir is the little clear plastic jar with the black cap, visible through the hole in the radiator wing.*

Replacing the brake fluid in either system is easy. At the caliper on either wheel, there is a bleed nipple. It usually has a small rubber cap over the nipple itself and a hex for a wrench below the nipple. Remove the reservoir cover or cap and top it off with clean fluid. Fit a clear piece of tubing over the nipple, this tubing should be long enough to go up from the nipple; 4-6 inches, loop over and reach down into a clean, empty container set on the ground next to the bike. With the correct sized wrench (do not use an adjustable wrench, you will ruin the hex on the nipple rapidly), break the nipple fitting loose to about a half turn and re-tighten it to barely snug. You will be loosening and re-tightening it often during this procedure. When the nipple is loose, the hydraulic system is open to the air. When it is tight, the system is sealed.

You can do the next steps yourself or with a helper. The goal is to build up pressure in the system by squeezing the lever or pressing the pedal (pumping may be necessary if the system has air in it). Hold that pressure by keeping the lever squeezed or the pedal pressed and then just opening the nipple, wherein the system's pressure will escape. Before the lever or pedal is released, the nipple must be closed again or the fluid and/or air that escaped will be sucked back in. Pump it up, hold, open nipple, close nipple, release.

By having the piece of tubing looped up and over, a small column of expelled brake fluid will stay above the nipple, lessening the chance of sucking air back in, and bubbles will rise to the top of the loop.

If you are removing air, you'll see the bubbles escape without a doubt. If you are flushing out old, burnt or wet fluid, you will clearly be able to tell when the new stuff makes it through the system.

CAUTION! Do not forget to check the reservoir nearly every cycle. You will be surprised by how fast this process works and how quickly you will run the reservoir dry. Only one squeeze of the lever or press of the pedal will suck air into the system if the reservoir is dry and then you have to keep cycling through the process until those bubbles are flushed out. I assure you that it is not uncommon to be almost done and then have to start over.

There are other methods and systems, including holding the caliper above the master cylinder and pumping new fluid in at the nipple and back up through the system.

## Cables

The cables on your bike need maintenance. They will get dirt and crud in them and will also eventually wear out. While some aftermarket designs are intended not to require lube, I have yet to find any cable that doesn't need this maintenance.

There are special lubes you can buy for your cables and there are indeed little clamp tools designed to ease getting lube inside, but you don't need either. Not to say that it isn't easier or that the purpose lube is not excellent! There is a picture of a cable luber in Chapter 2. With the cable end removed from its lever, the clamp serves to seal off the end of the cable's sheath, while supplying a small hole to pressure feed lube into.

First, disconnect the sticky cable from the lever or throttle (disconnect both ends of the throttle, so that you don't get a bunch of crud and/or lube into the carb). You can essentially wick lube into the cable/sleeve interface and pump/work it down the cable by cycling the cable in and out of its sleeve. If you have a sticky cable, you will know by feel when your lubing efforts have succeeded. I have successfully used a wide variety of liquid and aerosol type lubes in a pinch.

## Gear Oil

Modern bikes, in pursuit of minimum size and weight, carry a ridiculously small amount of engine oil, be they two or four stroke. This equates to the need to keep it very fresh. Higher quality oil (synthetic) certainly helps. In my bike, I'd run nothing else, even though no one has proven that regular change intervals with a quality petroleum based lubricant would fail to properly care for the engine. Follow your manual's instructions for changing the oil, including ensuring that you are using the correct viscosity and SAE or API rating. The drain plug is located underneath most two stroke designs, four strokers may also have them on the side. With a four stroke it would be wise to change the filter every time, too. Some bikes have ridiculously placed fill holes, so you may need a funnel. There are even specialty aftermarket products for the particularly difficult designs.

You must use an oil formulated for motorcycles. This is primarily due to the wet clutch all dirt bikes use, where the clutch is bathed in oil constantly. Automotive oils will probably lead to a clutch that slips. Another important reason, especially in a four stroke, is that the demands on the oil are very severe in a bike. The oil has to survive very high shear forces in the tranny, yet meet different lubrication scenarios in the cylinder.

Racers will change their engine oil as often as after every event. If your bike is lightly used and stressed, you might find that every six months or even twelve will do the trick. You might notice your oil's deterioration in harder shifting, rejected shifts, power loss and increased noise. Keep in mind, oil is very cheap compared to rebuilding your tranny and/or top end.

## Nuts 'n' Bolts

Fasteners are going to come loose - after all, what else could be expected from the pounding and vibration? You can either develop the habit of running through all of your nuts and bolts, or develop instead a habit of visiting your parts department for replacements (if you are lucky enough to only lose stuff and not have resultant crash induced damage).

If you constantly find a particular fastener coming loose, get a non-hardening thread locking compound and use it. In some cases a locking nut (nylock) is a good solution. Items like the kickstarter bolt are common candidates for thread locker.

Don't over-tighten stuff! You will strip threads - there is a lot of steel into aluminum and such. Or you will snap bolts and it is never fun extracting the remaining piece out of its threaded hole. Your manual has a torque table; use it.

## Engine

Your engine will wear out. Get over it. Your maintenance habits may be anywhere along the spectrum between keeping it fresh, to running it until it breaks hard or becomes essentially one piece of metal. I recommend that you tend toward the former, insisting that in the end it is cheaper cumulatively to keep it relatively fresh than to pay the face cost of rebuilding after a catastrophic failure.

The key metric for a two stroke is compression. A thread-in (preferable) or rubber-tipped press in compression gauge goes into the spark plug hole. The spark plug cap electrode (or the plug installed into the cap) is connected to ground (a good idea any time you turn over an engine with the plug-cap system not installed), the throttle is held open and the engine is kicked or cranked over until the needle goes no higher.

A brand new (broken in), water-cooled two stroke will hit at least 180 psi. I have seen them as high as 210. Once they drop below 150, a teardown had better be in your near future. An air-cooled two stroke should hit at least 150, and 120 should be your lower limit. The difference is in the tighter tolerances the engine can be built to given the superior temperature control of liquid cooling. Small bore engines that rev higher wear out faster than larger bore engines and riding skill and style play into engine life (as does air filter maintenance, correct jetting and no air leaks in the intake system). The engine oil in a two stroke only lubricates the transmission and has little if any effect on the life of the components in the cylinder. I have never seen a two stroke bike of any size run well, if at all, below 90 psi.

It is said, and I have often observed, that a two stroke's performance follows this life – power model. Brand new, broken in, they are at their peak. There is a rapid deterioration, but the change is minimal over the first day or three of use depending on the nature of the use. That is why top pro racers simply use a fresh engine every race – they can tell the difference. To wit, my '74 TM125, even with fifteen thousand milled off the head, was not known as a particularly fast engine. The Elsinores, Bultacos, Pentons and Kawasakis would regularly beat every Suzuki and Yamaha up Saddleback's famous start hill, every time. When I first raced it (my first real mx racing), by the time my skill at operating that bike was using everything it had to offer, the engine simply couldn't get me through the first turn in the first group. Thankfully it braked, handled and turned excellently and I could get up to 5th Junior by the end of each moto. Then I rebuilt the top end and almost got the holeshot at the very next race. It was back to 20th place starts three races later.

The engine will then stay at that level of performance for a relatively long time. Then it will seem to get faster! That means, in no uncertain terms, that it is at the end of its useful life and will start to lose major power and greatly increase the risk of catastrophe in very short order.

Keep in mind that if you keep your rings fresh, your piston will last longer. Keeping your piston tight will save your cylinder walls. Change the top end bearing, wrist pin and both circlips every time you change your piston.

By the way, your compression ratio is nothing more than how many times 14.7 (standard air pressure at sea level) divides into your engine's compression reading. So a 150 psi engine has about a 10:1 compression ratio.

The older designs of four strokers, almost all air-cooled, tend to be fairly mildly tuned and low stress engines that seemingly last forever and likely will with regular oil changes, clean air filters, properly adjusted valve lash and limited abuse. The newer, water-cooled, high performance engines that first appeared with the YZF400 are another story. The life remains driven by hours of use, type of use, air filter cleanliness and, for these engines, never-fail engine oil changes.

From what I hear so far about these new four strokes, they have a life – power performance curve that is barely noticeable, if at all. They just go hard until they blow, especially the 250s and they blow hard. I am aware of dealers that will not take them in trade unless they have an aftermarket hour meter installed (a very, very good idea, apparently). The piston and rings last fine. It is the valve trains that turn fragile. Just a severe over-rev, like from being in too low a gear landing a long jump, can shatter things.

A seized two stroke, including the worst case of having to buy a new cylinder, will set you back around $750 in parts. A blown-up modern four stroke can easily run you over two grand. Every honest mechanic will strongly recommend that you only run one so long and then rebuild it regardless of how well it is running.

## Clutch

As the clutch is designed to be slipped as necessary, not to mention handle tremendous loads, it will wear out. The basic thing that goes are the plates, especially the non-metal ones (these alternate with metal ones in the clutch basket). If your metal ones are aluminum, they tend to wear fast as well and you will see the shiny metal particles in your drained oil. You have to remove an access cover or the whole right side case and get into the clutch basket itself. There are too many variables from bike to bike to attempt an overview process in this book. Do change to steel metal plates when you rebuild if your bike didn't come with them - most non-OEM rebuild kits automatically include them. Ditto the springs, replace them when you rebuild. They're cheap.

If you think your clutch is failing (slipping), the easy test is to shift to third or fourth at what would be a low rpm for that gear and twist her wide open. The engine will clearly rev faster than it should, a lot faster, vs. the bike's acceleration. It may even break completely free and you'll slow down as the rpms head for the limiter. Other clutch failure symptoms tend to involve observations of notchy or hanging-up operation, which probably points to wear problems on the clutch basket itself.

## Coolant

A 50-50 mix of distilled water and aluminum radiator-friendly antifreeze is the typical manufacturer's recommendation. Keep a bottle of this mix in your box of bike fluids. Pop the cap before every ride and don't just look at height (indicative of leakage or loss in the cylinder), also look for foreign matter and discoloration, sure signs of trouble elsewhere.

## Bearings In General

The basic set of bearings you need to be concerned with other than those in the engine are front wheel, rear wheel, steering, swingarm and suspension linkage (including top and bottom shock mounts).

You will be more likely to have to work with your bearings if you ride in wet or muddy regions vs. dry or desert environs (but the latter have to clean air filters all the dang time, so it balances out).

Unfortunately, the manufacturers probably take the bearings as delivered by their suppliers and dealers generally make no changes, which means minimal and not particularly high quality grease was installed. You will be happier and your wallet heavier, especially in wet or muddy regions, if you tear down and repack all of your bearings with high quality, water proof grease, before you ever ride it.

The bearings are either "ball" or "roller" (like thick pins). These load-carrying, rotational balls or rollers ride on "races" (inner and outer). There is some type of integral seal or shield to both keep grease in and dirt out. The seals are not perfect, so water gets in and grease can leak out.

## Wheel Bearings

Wheel bearings are the interface between the axle and the hub. There is typically one per side of the hub, except at the sprocket side of the rear where there are often two, side-by-side. They are always ball bearings. They can be inspected after the wheel is removed from the bike.

*Gently prying off the outer seal.*

First, if there is an outer seal, not part of the bearing, you need to remove it. Slide a small flat blade screwdriver under the seal, approaching from the open axle opening. When you hit the metal surface associated with the outer diameter of such a seal, rotating the screwdriver will lift the seal out. Move around the seal and do this bit by bit. Made of fairly sturdy rubber, their real job is to seal against the axle only, so they have a fragile lip style seal at their inner diameter. A spring inside works to keep that lip pressed against the axle. Clean it all up real good.

Stick your finger in the hole of the now-exposed bearing and rotate the bearing's inner race. You will be able to feel anything other than smooth operation. If they feel gritty, debris is getting in the way of the balls or rollers. They may feel dry, then grease actually impedes movement at very slow rotation speeds. You may be able to feel looseness if they are significantly worn, or you might find you can hardly turn them, if at all, especially on a used bike where the owner never touched them (the leverage the diameter of the wheel has will make them roll, but your finger in the middle can't).

*Very gently lifting out the bearing's shield.*

You can remove the shields (these are not seals), which are like very thin, flexible flat washers with a rubber coating that snap into the zone between the inner and outer races, covering the balls. Use a very small screwdriver and approach from the ID. They lift out very easily. If you bend one, you can bend it flat again.

Look at the grease. Is it clean? Are they full? You can simply cram more grease in, with the bearing in place. Use your finger to lay a bead of grease all around the area between the races. Then rotate the inner race and watch the grease "disappear" into the bearing. They can hold a surprising amount. Keep adding it until no more gets sucked in, then re-fit the shield and clean up all the excess.

If they are dirty but appear to be otherwise serviceable, you'll need to drive them out in order to properly clean and repack them. First, if there is a circlip holding a bearing in, that will have to be removed. A long punch and firm hammer strikes, coming through the other side of the hub and working around the inner race, will drive a bearing out without hurting it. Don't drive the punch into the ball zone. You'll find a piece of pipe "floating" in the middle of the hub, especially on the rear, on many bikes. It moves out of the way enough to get the punch on the inner race (you will forget to put this tube in the first time you remove/replace bearings and then have to take one back out). Clean out all mating surfaces in the hub.

*You can get more grease into a bearing than seems possible.*

Once the bearing is out, remove both shields and use solvent or even compressed air to get them spotless. Examine them closely. If they don't look like new, but have no pitting on the balls or rust anywhere and spin free and tight, go ahead and reuse them. If they don't, replace them while they're already out. Notice how freely they spin without grease.

*Driving out worn old wheel bearings.*

There is a bearing packing tool you can buy and it works very well, but it is not hard to pack them full by hand. Install the shield on one side, lay on the beads of grease, spin them to suck it in, and repeat until full. Install the other shield.

Very carefully, working your way around the outer race, tap them back in. An old trick is to shrink the bearings slightly before attempting installation by sticking them in the freezer for four hours or so. Reinstall any circlips and outer seals and ride with confidence.

For almost all bikes, the wheel bearings are a standard item. This means you can pay your dealer additional profit for buying them and stocking them for you, or you can cut out the middle man and go straight to a bearing house. They will be far cheaper and you can opt for higher quality units as well.

**Steering Bearings**

These are not easy to inspect or service, but it is doable if you are a decent mechanic. You have to loosen the top triple clamp bolts (they hold the upper fork legs to the triple clamps) and possibly spread the clamp slightly with screwdrivers. There are nuts and such and a seal at the top of the steering stem which have to be removed. With the top triple clamp off and out of the way, the top steering bearing is exposed. Fortunately, a variant of the roller bearing called the tapered roller bearing is fairly common. Before these, loose ball bearings were employed. I still keep a couple of film cans with two common sizes of such, because it is almost impossible to not lose at least one during service.

Don't grease the top one yet, though. The bike has to be on a stand so that you can let the front wheel, forks and lower triple clamp drop slightly out of the steering stem to expose the lower bearing. Then you can pack it with grease, set the assembly back up into place, pack the top bearing and reassemble the upper triple clamp. The spanner nut (big square teeth around the outside) is used to adjust the load on these bearings. You want to get it snug, but do not over-tighten. If you can feel each roller as you slowly move the bars, it is too tight. Another test, with the front wheel off the ground, is to gently push on either end of the bars, starting with the wheel centered. This push should result in the bars moving to the stop, slowly. If it swings fast and bounces off, you're probably too loose. If it tends to resist swinging all the way, too tight. There should also be no up and down play you can feel in the system. Torque everything else per the numbers in your manual.

One little tip. Do not feed your tank's breather hose down the hole in the center of the steering, if there is one. The fumes are enough to break down the grease over time.

Once you have ensured that your steering bearings are fully lubed, as long as you don't blast it out with a pressure washer or the coin-operated car wash wand, they will last a long time, even years.

## Swingarm Bearings

Your swingarm pivots on long, skinny roller bearings called needle bearings. If you let these get too far gone, you will have a minor nightmare on your hands. It generally takes a press to get the races out. I have saved some pretty far-gone needle bearings, but not without hours of grief getting them clean, moving again, lubed and almost always, finding the ones dropped and getting them all back in place again. Lube these up real good while they're new. Stay on top of them if your steed sees lots of mud and water. Some install a zerk fitting (and some bikes come with them) so that you can regularly pump more grease in. If they are worn or failing, you can tell with the rear wheel off the ground. Grab the tire and move it side to side and try to twist it. You can easily feel play at the swingarm if they are starting to fail.

## Suspension Linkage/Shock Mount Bearings

These are mostly roller or needle bearings, except upper shock joints which tend to be a heim fitting – a special bearing comprised of a single large ball inside an outer race, where the mounting bolt is the inner race. These provide another degree of freedom besides axial rotation (of which there is very little required) and allow significant movement in all directions, allowing the shock to flex and not have to stay in perfect alignment with the frame. The needle bearings are either caged (easy to remove), or loose (meaning that they are held by the race and can only be removed by popping each out of the race or pressing the whole race out).

All of these need to be well-greased and maintained. They all have some form of rubber seal, none of which work perfectly and some seemingly not at all. For example, '98 KX250 owners always kept a bottom shock mount caged needle bearing in the toolbox because the $8 part failed so quickly in muddy, wet conditions.

Once the rear wheel is removed, you can attack the suspension linkage bearings one-by-one as you simply work through unbolting them. Make sure you torque every one back up to your manual's specs, since having any of these come loose (nylock nuts are commonly used) creates an easy-to-imagine disaster.

# Emergency Trail Repairs

Here's a quick list of common and not-so-common trail mishap damages and what you can do about them.

## Bars Out of Alignment

This typically happens because of a crash. If nothing is actually bent, including the bars, straddle the front wheel with both legs and jerk the bars back into alignment. The forks rotated within the triple clamps and they will generally be easy to jerk back into alignment. If the bars are not bent and you cannot get things to re-align, you may have bent the front axle or a fork tube.

If the bars are bent, you'll need a big piece of tree limb or a big rock, or a strong boot. Lay the bike on the ground bent end up and swing what you've got heartily at the end of the bars (the grip) in the direction needed to straighten them. I have never seen a throttle tube damaged by this, but I suppose that is a real risk. Your other choice is to continue with them bent.

*Squeeze the front tire between your legs, grab both ends of the bars and jerk them back into alignment with each other.*

*Set the bike on the ground, bars turned so they won't move any more as you whack at them, and go at it. A milk crate is being used here.*

## Flat Tire

If you don't have a patch kit, the needed tools and a way to inflate your tire, you can ride along as long as you can keep the tire bead seated on the rim. Wire or plastic ties spaced around the tire can help, but only if your right wrist stays mellow until you're back at the rig.

## Fouled Plug

If you don't have a spare, got a lighter or matches? Burning it dry sometimes does the trick.

## Broken Clutch Lever

On all cable-driven bikes and some hydraulic control sets, you can move the brake lever over to the clutch side. Of course, you will only be able to break with your foot. Or see...

## Broken Cable

Whether it is a clutch or throttle cable, a pair of vice grips attached to the upper broken end allows enough control to make it home.

## Broken Radiator Hose

Cutting it shorter and "stretching" it to fit is a possibility. Move the other end as far off its spigot as possible to help. Water from a drink system can be used to refill coolant temporarily. (You would not believe the fluids I have seen people use, including muddy water and urine, to get a bike out of the wilderness to safety.)

## Duct Tape

I have seen sticks and duct tape keep a broken handlebar together long enough for a gentle putt home. Heck, I have seen duct tape save countless dirt biking souls from disaster. It works to simply transfer your duct tape from its cardboard core to a handlebar or frame tube "core" and peel it off of there in an emergency. Duct tape is the best friend of every dirt biker on the planet, so never run out!

## Repairing Plastic

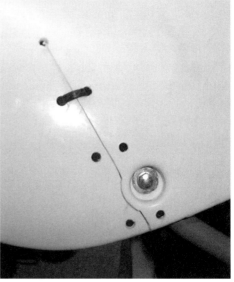

*This broken side number plate will hold up with this Frankenstein repair method. Note the hole drilled at the end of the crack to stop it from propagating, or growing. The zip ties go through the pairs of holes on either side of the crack. One black zip tie is installed in the upper set of holes for visibility in this picture, while the cleaner job attempts to match the color of the cracked plastic being repaired.*

There is a proven method of saving broken plastic if you can't afford a new piece. We're talking cracked plastic, the most common crash damage. First drill a hole around ¼" diameter at the end of the crack, so that the crack now "disappears" into the hole. This keeps it from propagating (growing). Next, you are going to "stitch" the crack together with plastic ties. Drill 1/8" holes in pairs along the length of the crack, about a ¼" from either side of the crack. Lace it up with the plastic ties. I have seen this last for years. For the trickest fix, use ties that are the same color as the cracked plastic.

## How to Get Gas From One Bike to Another

If you can obtain a useful container, simply remove your fuel line from the carb or petcock and transfer away. Usually though, the only containers are rider's drink systems and they are understandably resistant to the notion of adding gas to them. Disconnect both bike's fuel lines from the carbs (petcocks off) and

place the bikes side by side so that the ends of the two fuel lines can be butted up against each other. Press the ends together tightly and turn on both petcocks. The fuel will flow from the full to the empty tank, until both are at the same level. There will be some weeping at the joint you are holding together, but it's no big deal.

*To get gas from one bike to another, the petcock sides of each bike need to be as close as possible to each other.*

## Cleaning Your Bike

An old racing buddy once coined a phrase "A clean bike is the next best thing to a factory ride." I also had a friend who never cleaned his bike, except the air filter and chain, with the attitude of "It is just going to get immediatcly filthy again." I recommend keeping it clean. You can't spot damage or loose nuts and bolts, control's actuation can be hampered (interested in riding with a sticking throttle?) and wear on braking and drive train components can be increased.

She's your baby, right? Besides, you spend way more time caressing her with wrenches than your pavement ride (hopefully), you've got just the right stickers in just the right places, and you can't be fully proud as you pull up in the staging area unless she is gleaming like new.

The ultimate and easiest way to clean a filthy bike requires a pressure washer/coin-operated car wash wand/garden hose with sprayer attachment, a cleaning agent, a scrub brush, a plug for the exhaust and a bike stand. Here's the process, but if you use a pressure washer or the wand at a coin-operated car wash, do not ignore the CAUTION statements.

*There's a simple rubber stopper already in this silencer, and a specialty stopper complete with handle is also shown.*

- Plug the exhaust. This can be a simple rubber cork type, a trick item available in several styles at your bike shop, a can that fits over the end, or anything really, that will keep all water out of your exhaust.

- The first cleaning step is to get the big chunks off. The bike may not be "clean," but it will only be dirt "stained," not layered or buried. The cleaner cannot get to the interface between the bike's surfaces and the dirt, especially the stained sections, if you don't do this. Simply spray her down with whatever tool you have.
- CAUTION: There are a whole bunch of places where directing a high pressure spray will result in compromising the grease inside. Your o-ring chain is fine if you only aim at the side plates at a distance, but your steering, wheel, swingarm and rear suspension bearing areas are definitely NOT places to directly aim at! You have a couple of choices. If you are using a pressure washer, adjust the tip to a fan spray rather than a narrow jet. That lowers the pressure at any point the water hits. And/or, simply increase the distance between the tip and the bike. When I'm carving the thick goo away from under the fenders, I narrow the pressure washer to a jet. When I'm around bearings, the chain, or any stickers, I adjust to the fan and back away. At the carwash, distance is your only option.
- Start at the top and work down. A good order of locations would be: front number plate/handlebars, front fender, tank/seat rear fender, side panels/number plates/radiator wings, radiators, underneath the fenders, the front wheel, front of the engine, rear wheel and swingarm, sides of the engine, underneath the engine and lastly the rear suspension linkage. Having the bike on a stand makes it easy to spin the wheels to access all parts of them. Without a stand, you'll have to pause and roll her a bit to expose the hidden parts. Some lay their bike on its side to expose the bottom.
- TIP: You will get better at this, finding all the nooks and crannies, the approach angles to get at them, and how the mung you just blew off one section simply got redistributed on the section you just finished, with experience. There are also places that will get dirty that you cannot access without disassembly, including under the tank and sometimes between the skid plate and bottom of the engine as well as between the silencer and number plate.

A pressure washer makes cleaning a muddy bike easy, but be aware that the powerful jet can blow lubricant out of chains and bearings and graphics right off the bike. Compensate by keeping the wand a distance away from the bike and/or adjusting the wand tip for a fan-shaped spray rather than a narrow jet.

- Next, while the entire bike is still wet, spray it all down in the same basic order with a cleaner. Rotating the wheels as you spray makes it easy to evenly coat the spokes. Your bike shop probably offers several brands and they work fantastically, although they are more expensive than what you'll find at the hardware/grocery/automotive/big box store. My favorite for low cost, effectiveness and biodegradability, is green and leaves a pleasant pine scent emanating from your bike and making your garage smell better. If you buy it at a big box store, you get more than a gallon, plus an attached spray bottle full. You can cut it with water as recommended, but I think it does the best job undiluted.

*Using a garden type sprayer to deliver soap/cleaner to all parts of the rinsed bike.*

- TIP: Rather than blister your finger squeezing the trigger on the spray bottle, buy one of those pump garden/lawn sprayers. They hold nearly a gallon of cleaner, you pump them up once and can do the whole bike. The wand also makes it really easy to get the cleaner into every nook and cranny.
- TIP: The cleaners do not like direct sunlight. An overcast day does the trick, otherwise wash your bike in the shade, or move it to the shade as soon as you get it coated.
- Now let the bike sit for at least 15 minutes, preferably 30. This lets the cleaner really do its thing.

*A soft scrub brush isn't absolutely required, but it will ensure that most every stain comes clean.*

- If you must, take a scrub brush, spray some cleaner on it and gently massage the dirtiest areas. Yes, if you have white plastic on your bike this is probably required to get to "perfect."

- Now for the miracle. Rinse her, again in the same basic order. You will be amazed at how good the cleaner works – your bike will gleam, looking showroom new.

- Last steps now: post-wash lubrication. Apply a light oil to your kickstarter pivots and the folding tips of your rear brake and shift lever. Move them several cycles; you'll feel any grit "wash" out. Lube your chain. If it is an o-ring, "lube" it with a spray oil or o-ring chain lube spray. Spin the tire around a few times and the oil will displace any water and prevent rusting.

*Part of the post-wash lubing. An oil can is shown above at the kickstarter pivot, and below is a spray lubricant at the shifter tip.*

- It pays to lean the bike hard over and hold it for 10 seconds. Water will drip out of places where it would otherwise be trapped.
- Remove your exhaust plug, or you'll either be kicking and wondering why she won't fire or even more likely you'll spud-gun it across the yard into the bushes where the gremlins will hide it real good, lickety-split.
- Some like to start and warm the engine up completely, to finish drying it off. Some like to towel dry the major exposed surfaces.
- Never, ever, apply a vinyl protectant to your seat. You will either slide right off the back the first time you pin it, or plant the wrong part of your body firmly into the gas cap the first time you nail the brakes.
- You'll soon learn that the sooner you wash your bike after it becomes mud encrusted, the easier it is to get it off. It is getting ever more common to find racers figuring out how to get water into their pressure washer in the pits, so that they can get it done as easy as possible. You'll also re-discover "adobe," or why the builders who used mud bricks found them to be much stronger when laced with grass and other stringy vegetation. Indeed, you'll become quite the dirt connoisseur, noting those that wash easy or hard, which tend to stain and such. You may also find that you are creating a whole new sedimentary puzzle for some future geologist in the spot you always wash your bike.

## Tricking Out Your Ride

### Graphics/Stickers

There is quite an industry revolving around selling you different ways to decorate your bike. You can copy factory teams, jump maniacs or just go for a wild design. They'll sell you graphics for every square inch of your bike, with matching seat covers (changing one of those can be a real joy, but follow the instructions and you'll come out okay). There are gripper material graphics for the tank/shrouds… really, the assortment is ridiculously huge. Then there are stickers, of which there are literally millions.

Getting old stickers and graphics off ranges from simple to a nightmare. Sometimes the pressure washer will do it for you (whether you want it to or not). If I'm going to update stuff, the bike has to be super clean, so I'll narrow the jet and see if I can blow them off. After that, if I can't get a peel started by fingernail, a razor blade used very carefully will lift an edge safely. If it doesn't peel off cleanly, heat is your friend. A blow dryer works wonders. You are simply softening the adhesive so it will let go more easily. There are dumb sticker materials that just won't come off easily. The razor blade has to be used on every square millimeter. Or stop by the shop and buy some sticker removal chemical, which I have seen work on some tough ones.

Follow the instructions to prep the surface for application of new stuff. The most determined clean the surface with brake cleaner and then sort of "buff" it with a propane torch (careful!). If there are scratches in the plastic, likely as a crash is often the start of the death of a sticker or graphic, use the razor blade to scrape (not carve with the sharp point) the excess plastic away.

There are two schools of thought on applying, dry and wet. I have tried the wet, where you literally soak the surface and sticker with backing removed and "float" the thing into position, then squeegee the water out. I am not good at it. Dry, you peel away and fold back only a small portion of the backing and use the part of the sticker/graphic still covered by the backing to achieve proper placement. Holding it true, stick down the small uncovered piece. Then, working air out as you go, slowly peel away more backing and stick it down bit by bit. Plan your work across curved surfaces. It has always worked to re-lift a portion (immediately) if things go wrong and stick it back down. The side of the backing sheet that was against the adhesive seems to make a good pad to gently rub over the sticker to ensure it is down. Some use clear covers over rare or weak stickers. Clear nail polish around the perimeter has been used to help prevent peeling of stuff that seems susceptible.

*The "dry" graphic placement method, with part of the backing peeled away. The part of the sticker which still has its backing is used for positioning, the exposed part is placed down, then the rest of the backing is slowly peeled away while working the sticker down, eliminating air bubbles as you go.*

If you end up with an air bubble in the middle somewhere, prick it with a pin and work around the edges of the bubble to get the air out the hole you made. If you end up with a fold at the edge and the blow dryer and your fingernail won't iron it out, careful cuts down the center of the fold will result in new edges that line up, lay flat and resist peeling.

## Performance

There is no end to what you can buy for your bike to improve performance. I strongly recommend that you learn to ride the bike to its potential rather than waste your money, but we love to hotrod stuff so you're gonna blow the bucks anyway.

If you must spend money on improving your bike, start with the suspension. Find a tuner and work with them. Nothing will improve your speed more than maximizing the performance of your suspension vs. your skill, physique and typical riding scenario.

Then, if you must, go for engine improvements.

- These tend to start with the exhaust system, be it two or four stroke. But your best value may be elsewhere. Regardless, don't make your bike louder!
- On a two stroke, proper jetting (cheap), should be your first performance improvement step. On a related note, better reeds and intake tract flow boosters can have astounding results.
- Shedding unneeded weight should never be overlooked.
- Many intake or exhaust performance parts require that your bike be re-jetted.

Another improvement worth considering include adding a steering dampener. On some bikes noted for headshake under braking or acceleration, these are almost a must. But their ability to absorb impacts that might otherwise deflect the bike off line or rip the grips from your hand is real.

## Oversize Tanks

Typical motocross bikes do not have that much range. A two stroke 125 run aggressively might go 25-30 miles, a 250 perhaps another five more. Range for the 250 and 450 four stroke mx bikes will be yet a bit more. The off-road two stroke models have slightly oversized tanks that will get you 45-50 miles. Dual sport and the older air-cooled four strokes, if not ridden wide open, will easily exceed 50 and get out close to 90 miles. There are manufacturers of oversized tanks who do a great job of getting them to fit and hook up without major hassle.

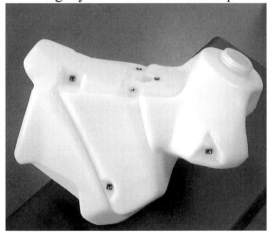

*An oversize tank.*

## Guards, Skid Plate

You can completely armor clad your bike if you wish. The two most common guards added are hand guards (still called bark busters, although that is a specific product name as well) and a skid plate. Naturally, the bottom of the frame/engine is the most vulnerable to rocks and other damage and that is what a skid plate can protect against. The good ones have extensions on the side to protect water pump housings. They are bike-specific, in terms of how they are mounted, access to engine oil drain plugs and fit. Another very commonly applied guard is a pipe guard. Two stroke pipes in particular are very vulnerable to rock and crash damage.

The two key styles are a relatively universal one that sort of looks like vertebrae/backbone and pipe specific designs that are essentially a second skin made from metal or Kevlar.

*An array of guards. Skid plates are to the lower left, a pipe guard to the upper right.*

The key to the universal one is to make sure, via slight bending of the wings along the edge, that the center sections are slightly elevated off the surface of the pipe.

Other types of guards are devices to protect your disk brake rotors, usually a full cover for the front and a blade-shaped piece commonly called a shark fin for the rear.

There are guards for most bar-mounted master cylinders and for the rear brake master cylinder.

*A pipe guard mounted up with long hose clamps.*

# Chapter 10

## *Talking Dirt Bike*

Now that you know how to dress, ride and maintain your bike like a real dirt biker, it is important to learn to talk like one. Below is a list of common terms you can use next time you are out on the trail or on the track.

**Berm** – In dirt biking, berms only exist in corners. They are essentially a wall of dirt shaped in a useful arc to help a rider guide his bike through the corner, hopefully quicker than could be done without one. When the Europeans first came to the US to teach us how to ride motocross (meaning "take all the available prize money while enjoying a vacation trip"), we watched them intentionally carve up berms in otherwise flat, groomed corners, using their bikes to do so. Usage these days seems to have been mangled, a berm being a man-made (as in bulldozer) arc'ed wall around the outside of a corner and the classic bike-created berm more often called a rut.

**Brakie** – The act of intentionally riding a motorcycle on the front wheel only. Powerful disc brakes combined with a very forward body position make these possible. Brakies, sometimes called stoppies, are generally considered to be an exhibition of bike control skill, rather than having any particularly useful function in riding or racing.

**Bulldogging** – A method of getting your bike down a hill so steep that you fear trying to ride it down. The bike is laid on its side, across the hill and pushed/slid down.

**Perch** – This metal part serves to mount the brake and clutch levers to the handle bars and provides the pivot point for lever movement. Also a scaly, bony and feisty but tasty fresh water pan fish.

**Poser** – Someone who has the latest, best equipment and gear, tricked out to the max and knows every last detail about every great rider, but can't ride to save his life.

**Quads and ATVs** – These are small four-wheeled off-road vehicles. All-terrain cycles (ATCs) are the three-wheeled versions, deemed so unsafe by the US government that their sale was banned.

**Roost** – Whatever the rear tire on the bike in front of you hurls at your bike, upper body and face. Back in the 70s, big bore Maicos were famous for brutal roost. I can personally attest to being pummeled with golf ball to baseball-sized clods and rocks from them on Saddleback uphills. Even with a chest protector, it hurt. They clearly "hooked up" with terra firma in an extremely positive way. Now, modern 450 and bigger four strokes are equally capable of hammering you.

**Sag** – This is a term associated with the basic adjustment of the rear suspension of a dirt bike. It is the difference between two measurements from the rear axle to a point above it, typically a spot on the rear fender. One measurement is taken with the bike's rear wheel suspended off the ground (which will be the bigger number). The second is taken with the rider astride the bike standing on the pegs (a smaller number, for sure).

**Spode** – A totally inept rider.

**Thumper** – An affectionate term for a dirt bike powered by a four stroke engine, derived from the pulsating, lower frequency sound they emanate, as opposed to the "ring ding" phrase oft applied to the two stroke motor's characteristic sound.

**Trick (Tricked Out)** – Has nothing to do with Halloween. Refers to very well-customized, performance-enhanced, visually-appealing and otherwise modified bikes.

**WFO** – There is one unspoken creed in the world of dirt biking, a pledge so deep that no one, anywhere, anytime, anyhow, has ever stated its official meaning, in print. At best, when pressed, a possibility or three might be offered, but confirmation of even the most insistent "guess" will be denied. Simply put, you either know what it means, or you don't.

**Wheelie** – The act of riding any vehicle on the rear wheel(s) only. This requires balance and throttle control to initiate and maintain. It is intended to help get the bike over a large obstacle such as a fallen tree or to "carry" the front wheel above and over water or mud, which helps keep the bike and rider clean and dry, or to show off. Wheelies can and do happen unintentionally - simply watch the start of any class short of pro at any race, as an example. These unintentional wheelies usually result in completely looping the bike out, wherein the wheelie motion continues to progress until the rider falls off the back and/or the bike's rear wheel passes under the bike's front wheel. The manufacturers of replacement rear fenders love these.

**Whoops (whoop-de-dos)** – successive, rolling, almost sinusoidal bumps (three or more). On modern tracks, these are completely man-made prior to a bike ever being ridden. They used to only occur naturally and are especially prevalent in the desert. Natural whoops are formed by the repeated action of the rear wheel under power, as initiated by a relatively small existing bump. The tire leaves the ground, gaining rpm before reconnecting, and that bit of wheelspin both starts to dig a hole and spits the dirt back at the first bump, tending to build it up. The natural oscillation of the suspension creates successive bumps. Each bike grows them more. Perhaps you've encountered "stutter bumps" on dirt roads only traversed by cars; these are the same phenomenon. Dirt bikes will also create another form of whoops, typically called braking bumps, on the approaches to corners. The term likely originated from the vocal response of the riders of early, poorly-suspended bikes as they pogo'ed through and across them. The singular is whoop.

# About the Author

*The author on his home track.*

Dad still laughs about the first time I got on a motorcycle. It was at a party at a racing buddy's home. (Dad raced sport cars nationally, even won a championship in '57 with an Alfa Romeo in SCCA B Production.) As motorsports enthusiasts will invariably do, the men ended up in the shop bench racing, brainstorming how to make the car faster, quaffing brewskis and telling jokes. As Dad's well-trained tool helper I was underfoot, about five, just hangin' with the guys.

Someone noticed the mini-bike in the corner. One of those lawnmower-powered, un-suspended, centrifugal clutch, flimsy framed, bench-seated ten-mile-per-hour wonders, it easily enticed them all to take a lubricated spin up and down the alley. With their bulk, ten miles per hour was more like five, but one would think it was 105 by the hooting and laughter.

Dad's buddy got the notion of putting me on it. I knew how to ride a bicycle, the brake made sense and the throttle felt natural under my palm. Down the alley I went and they couldn't get me off it. With my minimal weight, the thing relatively ripped and their next idea was to get me to wheelie. Just slide back, hit the throttle and pull on the bars, I was coached. It took a few tries to get the sequence together, but I got the front wheel up. The second time, veins now coursing with adrenaline, it came up easily and kept right on climbing, dropping me on my rear. The bike kept going, careened into a trash can and I think ripped out the throttle cable. I had some scrapes and bumped my head and Mom took over from a chagrined Dad.

To this day, I really don't like just doing wheelies. Oh, I'll pull the front up instantly and effortlessly if an obstacle like a log, ditch or water provides incentive, but it seems that any sort of show off wheelie for the heck of it results in damaged pride, body and/or bike. Example: Late 60s, San Felipe, in Baja, on my Dad's Suzuki 125 Duster, at the only intersection in town. Several slower friends just behind me, a significant crowd of locals and gringos all over the place. The Duster defined gutless and I knew it took liberal throttle and a dumped clutch to pop one. With the audience gawking at the gaggle of dusty kids poised at the intersection as though we were lined up for a race, a monster wheelie was required. Sure enough, I grabbed too much and came right off the back as the bike attempted to loop over. This was Dad's bike though and being naturally terrified of breaking it, I managed to keep my left hand (only) on the bars. Somehow, I ran after the bike, which dropped down and leaned left, bringing it around in a circle (still in gear and driving) and I somehow kept up with it until it happened to be pointed in the original direction and going slow enough to hop on. I actually got a big cheer but had to change underwear as soon as I got back to camp.

But I digress. From that first ride on, I was hooked, but there was nothing to ride. I was much too young to learn the Number One Rule of Dirt Biking: Never, Ever, Give Up The Bike You Have Until You Have Your Hands Firmly Around The Grips Of Your Next One (and its sister: It's Better To Own Two, Or More). Then my life of riding took off.

Dad, retired from racing and getting Phoenix International Raceway created, (which he designed and built and was certainly stressed by), got some seminal advice from the family doctor. The best way to relieve the stress you're under is to get a dirt bike and go riding with me and my buddies. Soon there was a used Triumph 200 Tiger Cub in the garage, a sale from a member of his new crew who was giving one of those new fangled two strokes, a Greeves, a try. They rode a lot, this pioneering squad. It seemed like every chance Dad could get, he'd be on it. We lived on the edge of the desert and he rode right from the house.

For me, I begged and got him to take me riding as often as possible. I'd mope when he went solo with the crew. Couldn't see a thing from behind him, couldn't reach around him, held on by sticking my hands in his coat pockets, but it sure didn't matter. We'd crash and I'd ride his back like a baby possum. He liked to "high mark" with me the most, point the little machine up and climb until traction or power gave out. Then we'd sit there and watch the colors of the sunset until it was time to creep back down and end Mom's worry about her boys somewhere out in the vast desert.

Dad hadn't learned the Number One Rule yet (I'm trying to save you some pain, okay?), but he finally got by the move to southern California, the new career (college professor), the broken washing machine, the blown transmission in the car and all those other things that Murphy will do pull to prevent you from getting another bike when you foolishly break Rule Number One. It was his favorite store, Montgomery Ward, which came to his rescue. In the mid 60s they sold Benelli's, Italian bikes with prized Ceriani suspension. The 260 four stroke was a bear to start and had a clutch that required championship arm wrestler hand strength to pull, but it was his pride and joy – like every dirt bike and every owner, ever.

Just entering my teens, I was just barely big enough to ride it. His rule was simple - if I could start it, I could ride it (when he wasn't). You'd dig deep and find a way too, I guarantee it. I quickly learned to find loops so I didn't have to slow too much and risk stalling the beast. His first attempt to put my own bike in the garage was another Benelli, a used 125 two stroke borrowed to "test," which was toast after only three days in Baja, somewhere near Ensenada. Okay, I'll admit to riding it dawn to dusk, everywhere, probably clocking more miles per day than a rider at the International Six Day Enduro. It died several miles from camp, but it was downhill for the first mile and it just coasted in.

So Dad convinced Mom that his 260 was "for the dirt, really, not good to run it only the two miles to work" and he brought home the Suzuki 125 Duster to commute to the college on instead (the Benelli was also a bear to start when cold). Now we could ride together. We benefited just like millions of families then and now. I passed my street license test and rode the wheels off the Duster. I was quickly into my own crew of fellow riders – you'll see how you gravitate together. My favorite days were at the old Saddleback Park. We would ride there, tanking up just before heading up Santiago Boulevard, strip off the lights, mirrors and turn signals and stash them in the bushes, ride all day, reverse the sequence and head home.

*Back when dirt bikes had exotic names, like this Ossa Stiletto. All fiberglass bodywork, including the tank, a double needle IRZ carb, and great power and handling for its time.*

Within a year, on the annual San Felipe Spring Break trip, Dad realized two things. First, I could disappear when we rode together, and second, I was going to do to the much more reliable Duster what I had done to the demo'ed Benelli 125. Back home, in short order there was a used '71 Ossa Stiletto, a Spanish bike, with the stipulation that all maintenance came out of my pocket. Now, I'd buy a clean '71 or '72 for pure nostalgia's sake, in a heartbeat. It was mine, my first real dirt bike.

I've only broken Rule Number One a couple of times since the Ossa and then ever so briefly. Off to college at MIT, the bike had to be sold. Three weeks later I found a Bultaco Matador ISDE Replica under a tarp in the fraternity garage. The owner said the magic words - get it running and ride it all you want. The colony of spiders banished, it took me barely twenty minutes to get the crud out of the carb, the plug clean enough and the motor running. I found another rider with two BSA 440 Victors. He taught me to call them Victims, because you had to own two to hope one would run. Not too many places to ride off-road in Massachusetts, but we still got our dirt miles in. Back home, I next owned two to make up for two years of not owning one and started my mx career. A soul-searching journey across this great land, ending with a wild two-year side trip to Puerto Rico, was also started bike-less. I snagged some rides here and there and stumbled on to a Honda MT Elsinore while in Puerto Rico from a wannabe whose wife was forcing him to give up after one gnarly endo. A neighbor who did custom Vette paint jobs on the island repaired the damage and painted her a deep candy apple red.

I have never broken the Rule since. What a train of bikes it's been. Let's see, a; 78½ Suzuki RM 250C2 (still have a piece of a fork leg – that was some crash), '83 RM250 with the '82 head (still competitively fast today), '87 KX250, '90 KDX200 (completing my transformation from a SoCal dez/mx rat to a NW woods trail rider), '93 Suzuki DR350S (the dual sport experiment that I modified extensively),'96 KTM360EXC (and street legal), '98KX250 (what a motor, hung on to that bike for a while), an '01 GasGas300 and that being the best bike I ever rode or owned, now an '04 GG300, again street legal. Hmmm, started with a Spanish bike, in love with them again.

Forty-eight years of dirt bikes. Married twenty-five years, just six weeks after meeting. My wife Joanne had been brought up around bikes; since we hitched up she has always had her own as well. Three children, Jessica, Cory and Jennifer. Riding dirt bikes has been incredibly good to and for our family. The kids know how to ride, they can take care of their bikes and cars, and they have become drivers who haven't gotten in accidents. We've looked out over fantastic vistas together, planned and gone on countless trips and spent tremendous time together as a family. And they have learned all the life lessons riding and racing have to offer.

I wouldn't change a second of my dirt bike history. Well, I would have learned Rule Number One sooner and I would have fought harder against some of those show-off wheelie urges.

I can't wait for my next ride. It will be an adventure!

And when you take that first ride, or your next one, it will be an adventure for you too - you'll see . . .